Bright Ideas
Teacher
Handbooks
Maths

Published by Scholastic Publications Ltd,
Marlborough House, Holly Walk,
Leamington Spa, Warwickshire CV32 4LS

© 1987 Scholastic Publications Ltd

Contributors: Geoffrey Matthews, Julia
Matthews, Beryl Webber, Jean Haigh, Nicola
Davies, Vivienne Jahans, Martin Blows,
Lesley Jones, Sally Dally, Ruth Merttens.

Edited by Priscilla Chambers, Jackie
Cunningham-Craig and Jane Hammond
Sub-edited by Melissa Bellamy
Photographs by Richard Butchins
Illustrated by Jane Bottomley and Roy Mole

Printed in Great Britain by Ebenezer Baylis,
Worcester

ISBN 0 590 70800 7

Front and back covers: photographs by Martyn
Chillmaid; styled by Sally Rowat; equipment courtesy of
E J Arnold & Son Ltd

Introduction

Why teach mathematics?

Mathematics has been described as 'the queen and servant of science'. One might well add 'and of the arts as well', as mathematics can be found everywhere. Sometimes it is difficult to recognise, as it includes not only traditional number work, but also logical thinking, the ability to solve problems, the study of measurement and space.

But why teach mathematics to young children? There are many answers to this question and perhaps the simplest is that it is part of their birthright. With each skill there goes one or more concepts. For example, the skill of counting depends on the concept of matching. This can be illustrated by a child counting his birthday cards. He holds up the first card and says 'one', then it is joined by a second card – 'two', a third card – 'three', and so on. This is matching the numbers to the cards and so gives a count of their number. However, failure to match properly leads to the numbers getting out of control with, for example, the sequence '1, 2, 3, 4, 5, 6' being gabbled while only four cards are held up.

A failure to grasp the concepts is just as disastrous as an inability to use the skills. If children learn everything by rote without understanding, sooner or later they will switch off. This leads to a second reason for 'doing maths' at school, namely to acquire the ability to solve problems in the world beyond the classroom. A child who has been allowed to 'slip through the net' and who ends up labelled 'no good at maths', will be very poorly qualified for the rest of his life.

Perhaps the best justification for including mathematics in the school curriculum is that it can bring pleasure. This may seem barely credible to past generations brought up on fear of being penalised for not knowing the tables or afraid to confess that they didn't understand the dreaded rules such as 'turn it upside down and multiply' or 'two minuses make a plus!' These fearsome slogans are gradually disappearing.

This doesn't mean that all the 'old' maths was bad. Quite the reverse. Even in the computer age it is still essential to know one's tables (if only to check the machine!). But there is more than one way of learning them, a remark which will be amplified later.

How to teach

It must be recognised that eventually mathematics is an abstract subject. No one has ever seen a 'two' but understanding the meaning of 'twoness' comes from much experience of duos – two apples, two pears, two cars . . . children in fact learn by *doing*, by actually handling the apples, pears etc. This is particularly true of young children but many adults do still understand better with something to handle. 'Teaching by telling' is therefore not enough.

Another factor in the classroom is that children are different and each learn at a different rate. Even in the most determinedly streamed class, the range of ability is great, and one child may be well ahead on spatial ideas or measurement, while his companion may be quite hopeless at geometry but able to make the most unlikely difficult computations. This makes 'teaching by telling' even more suspect as the main vehicle for learning. The chapter on 'Catering for individual children' (see pages 105 to 115) expands on coping with children of different abilities.

It is, however, dangerous to go to extremes. Children left indefinitely with a

Understanding of simple mathematical concepts is gained from first-hand experience in handling objects.

welter of apparatus are unlikely to discover many mathematical ideas or skills. An occasional talk to the whole class may well prove rewarding, particularly when introducing a topic new to everyone.

There are, unfortunately, no instant recipes for a successful teacher of mathematics, but as a general guide children should be put on the path of 'discovering' with as many hints as necessary. Once the penny has dropped it is time for reinforcement with some good old-fashioned practice.

Tables

The learning of tables serves as a good illustration of this principle. The whole class chanting 'one three is three, two threes are six' etc can only lead to disaster. If you were to ask adults at random in the street whether they liked mathematics at school, the vast majority would reply 'Ugh no, maths – those tables!' On the other hand, children who go on to secondary school without 'knowing' up to say ten time ten are at a serious, and quite unnecessary, disadvantage.

Tables can be built up slowly. Counting on, for example, in fours can lead to the pattern 4, 8, 12, 16 . . . and this is one step towards the four times table. Many different experiences are necessary: eg How many dots?

— — — — — — —

— — — — — — —

— — — — — — —

— — — — — — —

— — — — — — —

The child who 'knows' $6 \times 4 = 24$ (by cranking up from $6 \times 1 =$, $6 \times 2 = 12$ etc) but still has to count the dots one by one needs more such experiences, if necessary having the 'short cut' pointed out to him. After many experiences, the child can be encouraged to fill in as much of a table as he can: eg

X	1	2	3	4	5
5					
4	4				
3	3	6	9		
2	2	4	6	8	
1	1	2	3	4	

This leads to a challenge to know a few more, until the whole chart up to ten times ten is complete. Eventually, chanting can be quite a happy way of reinforcing – even by the whole class! By this time there is no fear, but understanding as well as recall.

Using symbols

Earlier it was stated that 'mathematics is an abstract subject', and the 'twoness of two' was given as a simple illustration. A more sophisticated example would be a statement such as:

$$3 + 4 = 7$$

This can be 'taught' quite meaninglessly with children not appreciating the meaning of any of the symbols. The acid test is to give the child three buttons and then four more and ask: 'How many altogether?' If the child counts in ones, and perhaps gets an answer such as six or eight, the 'knowledge' that $3 + 4 = 7$ is useless as it has not been transferred to the problem. A better way to proceed is to go slowly with the symbols. Plenty of experience with practical things (three buttons, four more buttons, altogether seven buttons etc) will one day convince the child

Maths opportunities arise out of simple activities.

that three of no-matter-what together with four of whatever-you-like gives seven objects altogether. That is the moment of abstraction (literally, the idea has been abstracted from the concrete experiences), when it is meaningful to introduce and indeed teach the written symbolism $4 + 3 = 7$.

Every mathematical discovery needs a welter of concrete experiences. These may sometimes be contrived with apparatus, but more often opportunities will arise from normal classroom activities.

For example, the length of a plant or classroom animal may be measured and recorded at regular intervals. Someone may bring in a collection of sea shells, which can be sorted in various ways as well as, of course, being counted. The children may go out for a walk, which can lead to the production of simple maps. The opportunities are endless. Further ideas are presented in the chapter on 'Maths within the curriculum' (see pages 13 to 22).

Language

It has been said that 'mathematics is a language'. Certainly mathematics *has* a language, and it must not be abused any more than English or any other language. For example, the plus sign should only be used between two numbers, and = (equals) between two sets of numbers which have the same sum (eg $3 + 4 = 7$ or $15 + 29 = 44$). During the transition stage from concrete to abstract it is difficult not to use expressions such as 'three and four make seven'; 'three add four gives seven'; 'three, four, altogether seven'. These, however, should be used sparingly as the same thing said in too many different ways can be confusing. Even '3 apples + 4 apples = 7 apples' is a nasty mixture of two languages. To use the sum '3 metres + 4 metres = 7 metres' applied to measurement made by children ignores the important question of the approximate nature of measurement.

There are some words which have different meanings in the real world and the world of mathematics: for example, 'pair' for 'pear', 'odd' for 'odd' (strange) and 'even' for 'even' (level).

To a young child size and magnitude

can also present problems: for example, a two drawn longer than a nine can mean that the two is the 'bigger number'. Another example is 'groups', which is probably best avoided altogether at primary school when it is really a question of 'sets'. Doubtless the reader can cite many more examples.

Geometrical figures ought to be introduced with their correct name so that they won't have to be unlearned later. A square should not be called a diamond just because it's drawn on its side (although young children are not always able to appreciate that it is the same shape). Again, there is little justification for calling a rectangle an oblong as if this were somehow cosier. By all means start with the child's own vocabulary but introduce the correct terminology alongside from the earliest stage.

Problems and projects

Children can be encouraged to think for themselves in a variety of ways. They will occasionally come up with their own problem:

How many squares are there here?

Such problems will, however, generally be suggested by the teacher. Having solved such a problem, the children should be encouraged to make their own generalisation: eg

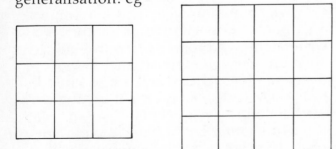

How many here?
Can you find a pattern?

Projects can often involve maths work.

Mathematics can also come out of project work which will often provide the much needed motivation and interest for many children. It is important that mathematics is not seen merely as a school based subject but that it applies to the outside world. Projects need not be sophisticated or ambitious – a simple event, followed by good teacher planning can lead to much enthusiastic work. For example, some very wet weather could lead on to a count and pictorial display of: wet weather clothing; shoe/boot sizes; colours of boots/macs/umbrellas/; measure of rainfall; comparison of maximum/minimum temperatures; weight of water; floating and sinking; uses of water; count of sinks in school/at home; recording favourite rainy day songs and the timing of singing them.

The chapters on 'Children as investigators (see pages 25 to 38) and 'Developing problem solving' (see pages 41 to 53) extend the ideas outlined here.

Communication

Through all the activities (practical work, problems, projects), it is essential for the children to record what they have done and state any relevant conclusions. Such recording may at first be made orally between child and teacher or child and the class, or it may take the form of a picture;

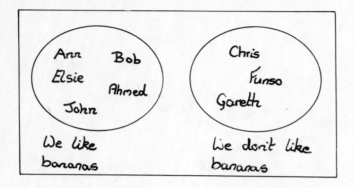

or later in the form of a graph;

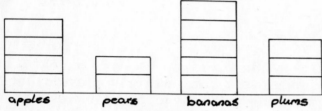

Bananas were the most popular
Five children chose bananas
Four chose apples
The least popular was pears

At a later stage more facts may be gleaned from the date:
We asked 14 children
$4 + 2 + 5 + 3 = 14$
$5 > 4$
$4 < 5$ etc
The same information displayed in three different ways is more rewarding (and less time-consuming!) than three pieces of information displayed in one way. 'Presenting results' (see pages 55 to 65) gives further examples and ideas.

Progression

Unfortunately perhaps for recording purposes, children do not learn neatly. An idea is often here today, gone tomorrow. Concepts, skills and acquisition of facts tumble over each other. This makes it essential to try to find out just where the children are in their thinking, so that relevant experiences can be provided for them. It is disheartening for a child to have to soldier on with something too familiar to him. But it is equally discouraging to be given a task way beyond one's grasp (eg 29 + 43 when the child has no idea of place value and may even be unable to compute 9 + 3).

Assessment should not be allowed to get out of control (and leave no time for teaching!) A good rule is to check upon a child's progress only when hearing oneself say 'I wonder if he really understands . . .'. The chapter on 'Evaluating children's progress' (see pages 93 to 103) contains many practical suggestions for assessing children's progress.

Computing aids

The hand calculator is clearly here to stay. It should not replace mental or written computation but can serve as a useful motivation and check.

The role of computers, however, needs special consideration. There has been a strong temptation for a school first to buy a micro and then to start wondering how to use it. Some very unsuitable software has been produced: for example, using the computer to set sums which would be more relevantly contrived by the teacher, or a display of cubes when the real thing would be much more appropriate. Another doubtful role for computers in schools is to provide games where the only skill needed is a lightning forefinger. On the other hand, there is some good software now available giving the children problems to solve as well as games requiring real thought to play. It is very difficult for the teacher to find time to preview programs and help must be given, perhaps on an area basis.

Even more importantly the computer can offer the opportunity for the children to write their own programs. Even an apparently trivial exercise, such as getting the computer to display all the odd numbers from one to fifty, can give real creative satisfaction.

The chapter on 'New technology' (see pages 67 to 90) will help you to make the best use of calculators, computers, and even digital watches in the classroom.

Software needs to be chosen carefully to ensure that children are practising skills.

Choosing a scheme

As emphasised in the Cockcroft Report, published schemes of work can only reinforce and there is no substitute for practical experiences organised by the teacher. On the other hand, it is no solution to use a variety of schemes picking out the more attractive fragments. 'Structuring your programme' (see pages 1 to 11) outlines the areas which any mathematical programme should cover.

The key points to note when choosing a scheme are as follows:
● Does it cover your range of age and ability?
● Does it encourage practical work before doing the examples?
● Is it mathematically sound?
● Does it cover at least most topics laid down by your LEA?
● Is it cost effective? (eg Does it avoid expensive, disposable workbooks?)
● Is there too much reading required by the children?

● Does it give guidance on progression, assessment, record-keeping and practical suggestions for children who need more help?
● Above all, will it help the children to find pleasure and enjoyment as well as achievement in mathematics?

Involving parents

More and more these days parents are taking an active role in their children's education. Schools encourage parental participation in a variety of ways – as school governors, fund raisers, and classroom helpers to name but a few. Many involve parents in 'shared reading' schemes which have proved very successful. Mathematics up till now has been an area where parental help has often been actively discouraged. But the climate of opinion is slowly changing. The chapter on 'Involving parents' (see pages 117 to 124) gives further information.

Structuring your programme

Structuring your programme

INTRODUCTION

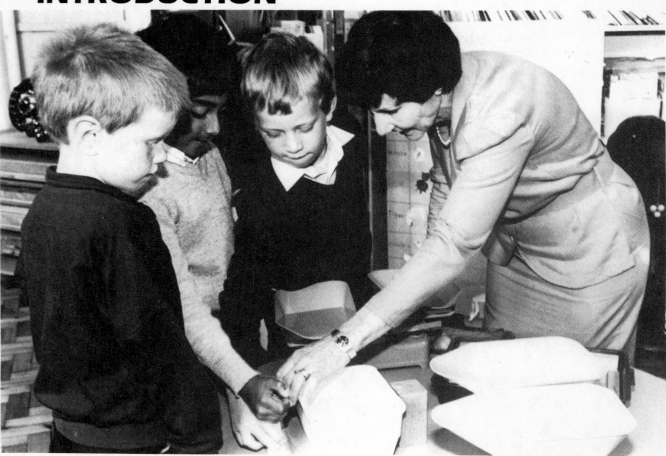

Why examine the school's mathematics programme at all? Why not just follow a published scheme? The answer to the first question is that mathematics is essentially an ordered activity and without structure there is a danger of losing progression in a mass of detail. It is essential to know where each child is going and to be aware of the relevant experiences which will take him on the next stage of his mathematical journey.

Children are individuals and this partly answers the second question. No published scheme can ever be devised which caters for a whole class with all their different needs and abilities. Again, mathematics is not learned from workbooks, cards or sheets. These can, of course, provide good back-up

and practice, but the actual learning by young children comes from their own experiences, from handling a variety of materials until finally the underlying mathematics comes to the surface. The materials are, of course, structured by the teacher with whom discussion is essential in order for 'the penny to drop'.

Apart from the children and the mathematics, there are other factors to be considered, namely the LEA, the teachers, the environment and principles. Most LEAs have devised guidelines (as now demanded by the DES) based on the excellent DES papers, *Mathematics from 5 to 16* and *Mathematics 5–11*. These guidelines are broadly outlined in this chapter.

Teachers should not work in isolation, so involvement of all is essential when planning any programme, particularly one as complex as mathematics. Trying to get suggestions and ideas from all the staff is a lengthy business but time is saved in the long run by lessening the need for explanations at staff meetings. Such meetings are still essential for the exchange of ideas and experiences and school guidelines can be discussed and kept under review. Parents' meetings can be planned to try to ensure common ground on expectations. It may even prove useful at times to set up working parties to consider particularly contentious topics or review new commercially produced materials.

As for the environment, this should have a crucial effect on the curriculum. The local history, buildings, streets, houses and shops are all possible grist to the mathematical mill. For example, a short walk to the post-box with a 'get well' card for a sick classmate could provide plenty of mathematical fodder:
What time did we start from school?
What time did we arrive back?
What time would the card be collected – morning or afternoon?

Learning needs to be based on the child's experiences.

How long was our journey?
How many cars/bicycles/prams/people did we pass?
How many roads did we cross?
What were the numbers on the doors (odd/even, or less than 20)?
How many children/adults went to post the card?
Were there more boys/girls?
What shape is the 'get well' card?
What shape is the stamp/envelope?
What shapes have we seen on our walk (windows/doors/chimneys)?
Draw a plan of our route – what were the names of roads/streets?
Which road/street had the most letters in the name?

After such an outing, enthusiasm and other commitments will determine how far the work goes. Certainly a great deal of pictorial representation and calculations could arise which are entirely child-centred, but the structuring must come, initially, from the teacher.

When planning the mathematics programme, there are certain principles to be borne in mind. For example, the *early stages of* learning mathematics are of crucial

Each child has individual needs and abilities.

3

importance for laying sound foundations. These early stages should not be sacrificed because of pressure, from whatever source, for the pupils to do written exercises as 'proof' that they have 'done' some mathematics. There is far more to mathematics than marks on a piece of paper. There is sometimes a very strong temptation in the early stages for schools to go for superficially quick progress in written work *before* conceptual understanding is sufficiently well established. Indeed some young pupils are still struggling to form the figures whilst writing sums, and premature symbolism is known to be counterproductive. The principle of accepting a slow progress in the written work in the early stages will ensure that subsequent progress can take place confidently and often more quickly. All pupils benefit from appropriate practical work, not only in the early stages and irrespective of their ability, be it bundling sticks into tens or structural apparatus for place value, throwing dice for probability data, making mathematical models or measurement in all its forms.

There are times when the teacher needs to explain, to stimulate and activate pupils and above all to discuss the mathematics they are doing. The quality of pupils' mathematical thinking as well as their ability to express themselves can be considerably enhanced by discussion (not monologue!). Indeed, it is mainly through discussion and practical work that teachers will understand why errors are made and what steps are needed by particular pupils to clear up confusions.

Bearing all this in mind we can look at the mathematical content which should be considered under the following broad headings: aims, objectives, criteria for content, classroom approaches and assessment.

Aims

There must be aims for all pupils although the way they are implemented will depend on ages and abilities. It is important that children learn, from the earliest stages, that mathematics is a powerful means of communication. The *aim* must be to convey meaning and if pupils cannot interpret the result of a mathematical task, then it has little value for them, mathematically speaking. For example, if a pupil is able to perform successfully a subtraction sum but is not able to determine whether the answer

Children will find practical work helpful at every stage and written work should not be forced.

is reasonable or to transfer the operation to another situation, then the 'learning' that has taken place is only instrumental. The aim must be for relational learning and using mathematics as a tool in a wide range of activities at school and later in adult life.

Pupils may not be given the opportunity to appreciate these relationships if they are too preoccupied with trying to master the details. The order, pattern and relationship of numbers appeal to many, if not all, children and this appeal should be fostered as an ingredient towards the aim of achieving numeracy.

At every stage pupils should be entitled to feel confident in the tasks they are given – repeated failure should *never* be allowed and careful matching of tasks to ability should ensure this confidence. No pupil, however young, should be allowed to think of himself as 'no good at maths'. On every possible occasion pupils should be encouraged to talk about their mathematics, sometimes in pairs, sometimes in small groups or to a larger audience and sometimes with their teacher alone.

Children need to be encouraged to discuss their work, revealing problem areas and increasing confidence.

Objectives

Having considered the wider aims of the mathematical curriculum, these can now be followed through into more specific objectives. There are five main categories, each of equal importance and each to be considered in conjunction with the others:
- the assimilation of concepts,
- the acquisition of facts,
- the development of skills,
- the facility for making sound strategies,
- the enhancement of personal qualities.

Each objective is an essential part of mathematics and must be given serious consideration when structuring the programme. Concepts, facts and skills are very closely knit and not much use to the pupil one without the other.

Concepts

Concepts make up the substance of knowledge which leads to relational understanding and on to the transfer of a concept from one situation to a seemingly different one. An example is afforded by any one of the 'four rules'.

The concept of addition is abstracted from many experiences of finding the total collection. For example, four apples, three more apples – seven altogether. Eventually the children will realise that four of any object with three other objects (no matter what) give seven altogether. The acquisition of the concept includes a realisation of *when* addition is relevant and the child doesn't have to ask the classic question 'Is it an add, Miss?'

Facts

Facts need to be learned: for example, a pupil might forget the result of $11 + 10$ but if he has understood 'one more' and has learned that $10 + 10 = 20$, then he can quickly deduce $11 + 10$.

The application of learned facts should take place at every opportunity: for example, instead of allowing pupils to go on using counting aids (and so encourage counting in ones) when simple number bonds are put to them, all means should be employed to get them to recall and apply what they know.

Skills

Skills include not only the use of number facts and standard computational procedures, but the sensible use of a calculator and the skill of measurement. Oral skills in maths should be encouraged, as should the skill of communicating and explaining results, a description of methods used in solving a problem and the skill required for interpreting a graph. It cannot be stressed often enough that *skills are not ends in themselves.*

The ability to decide which skills to use and what areas of knowledge to apply is vital.

Sound strategies

These include the ability to estimate, to appreciate the approximate nature of all measurement, to reason, and to look for pattern. To quote *Mathematics Counts* (Cockcroft Report): 'General strategies are procedures which guide the choice of which skills to use or what knowledge to draw upon at each stage in the course of solving a problem or carrying out an investigation.'

Personal qualities

Personal qualities may be summed up quite simply as the development of good work habits, not least in mathematics. Such habits should be fostered in the classroom approaches and by a positive attitude towards mathematics. For example, if the mathematical task is relevant (as indeed it *should* be), then confidence in an ability to fulfil that task and the satisfaction derived from a sense of achievement will help to cultivate positive attitudes. It must always be remembered that *all children are different and progress at different rates.* There are slow thinkers and slow movers who are nonetheless mathematically able, given time. It is not always the pupils with the ready, rapid replies, sometimes incorrect, who make the best mathematicians.

Criteria for content

With these general objectives in mind, the next task is to choose the appropriate mathematical content of the school's programme. This content needs to be chosen so that the pupils can cover it successfully at their own level. This means that *all* pupils should be challenged but in such a way that they do not meet with continual failure. Time must be allowed for much practical work and discussion, even if this results in a reduction in the range of the syllabus.

The content should not be a collection of unconnected items, but should be designed as a network of whole relationships. The aim is that all pupils should be enabled to appreciate the structure of the mathematics they have done, and understand the relationships between particular concepts. Although the range of the content may be reduced, perhaps to include more time for practical work etc, nevertheless it must be sufficiently broad for *all* pupils. For example, the least able should *not* be reduced to number work only, but work on space, shape and measurement should come together quite naturally with a numerical content. Above all, mathematics must be placed in context with the whole curriculum – project work, science, games, music etc.

The main content of the curriculum is traditionally under four headings: sets, numbers, shape and space, and measures.

Sets

Sets are not dealt with separately here because they pervade the whole of mathematics: there are sets of numbers (eg the primes – 2,3,5,7,11 etc), there are sets of shapes (eg 'from this set of shapes sort out the right-angled triangles'), and there are

Pupils must be able to achieve success.

sets of measures (eg the heights of the pupils in the class).

Numbers

Numbers are encountered by children long before they come to school, for example, on buses and front doors. The task of the teacher of the youngest pupils is to build on these encounters at whatever level has been reached. The following is a sequence in the development of number in the primary school:
● Familiarity with the numbers 0 to 9, including comparisons, ordering, matching in one-to-one correspondence, conversation, and fluent writing of symbols.
● Addition of pairs of numbers (single digit).
● Extending experiences to numbers with two (and later more) digits. The difficulty of place value is often underestimated: for example, why should 13 mean one ten and

three units to a child, rather than 31 or 4? The convention is not necessarily obvious and many concrete experiences are needed.

● The four rules ($+, -, \times, \div$) gradually and separately built up to cover larger numbers. It is essential that the idea of addition is well understood before the other operations are introduced formally.

● Fractions and decimals. Starting with motivating activities such as cake-sharing (½, ¼, ¾) and leading on eventually to simple addition of the abstract numbers: ½ + ¼ = ¾. Simple equivalents: ½ = 0.5, 1½ = 1.5. Money sums can be used to illustrate the more formal manipulation of decimals (1.55 + 2.13 is a mathematical model for £1.55 added to £2.13, which may be meaningful earlier).

● Throughout all number work, free use should be made of the hand calculator, especially for the pupils to check their own calculations and for investigating numbers and operations.

● Mental arithmetic is also invaluable. For example, encourage children to add 3 to 8 by starting from the 8 and counting on '9, 10, 11' instead of going back, literally, to square one (1,2,3 etc).

● At all levels there are patterns and relationships between numbers to be discovered and learned (for example, recognising the repeating pattern of 5 + 10 = 15, 15 + 10 = 25 etc, and the commutative relationship of $4 \times 2 = 2 \times 4$).

● Finally, estimation should be encouraged whenever possible. For example, 29×61 is approximately 30×60 (1800) so if the pupil's answer contains three or even five digits, he has obviously made a mistake and has the opportunity to think again.

Allow children to use calculators to investigate numbers and operations and to check their work.

Shape and space

Well before children start school, they are involved in both shape and space. They develop an awareness of many shapes around them, from their toys, the bric-a-brac they find in park or garden, and the plates, pots and pans that surround them daily. They are involved in space from the moment they are born, exploring the environment and their own position and mobility in it. Teachers need to develop the early natural curiosity aroused by shape and space throughout the school years. An order of development may be structured along the following lines:

● Free play and informal examination of 3-D shapes, both man-made and natural, touching and talking about them.

● Sorting 3-D shapes (including ones with holes in them) according to the children's criteria.

8

● Making patterns from shapes, such as potato prints.

● Drawing round the faces of 3-D shapes and in this way abstracting 2-D shapes from them: for example, tracing round one face of a cube, obtaining a square.

● Modelling solid shapes in clay etc, and constructing, for example with bricks or Lego.

● Further sorting, discriminating between attributes, describing shapes and looking for differences and similarities.

● Exploring space, by fitting 3-D shapes together, and covering 2-D plane surfaces with different shapes, with and without overlap.

● Giving pupils opportunities to explore line symmetry (balanced shapes), making 'blob' patterns by using folded paper, cutting patterns, using mirrors to produce symmetrical patterns.

● Extending the classification of shapes: for example, right-angled isosceles triangles.

● Using a pair of compasses for circle patterns.

● Exploring shapes with the microcomputer.

● Considering angles through turning by working with clock faces, wheels, pendulums etc.

● Measuring angles in simple terms by using right-angles, or half- and quarter-turns.

● Exploring regular and irregular solids.

● Considering skeleton models of 3-D shapes and rigidity.

The potato prints mentioned as an early activity can be used at a different level later to introduce the idea of a translation: that is, a pattern being repeated at regular intervals. If the potato prints are made end-to-end they can also be used as a simple introduction to measurement: 'The table is about 12 potato prints wide.'

The work with angles described leads to the idea of a rotation, while that in symmetry leads on to reflection (for example, in a mirror). Thus the primary syllabus described leads to the three major geometrical concepts encountered later of translation, reflection and rotation.

Finally, it is important to realise that some children are more agile with numbers while others are more naturally at home with spatial properties. This should be taken into account when structuring the programme.

Include work on shape and space in your programme.

Measures

There are two types of quantity: discrete quantities which are counted, and continuous quantities, such as length, weight, volume and surface area, which are measured. The main measures in primary school are length, weight, capacity and volume, area, time, angle and temperature. The approximate nature of measure must at all times be stressed: for example, it is correct to say that a piece of ribbon measures 'between 10 and 11 cm' and that 'Jane is about ½ cm taller than her friend'.

Before the introduction of any numerical measure, activities to reinforce the following stages should be experienced:

● Direct comparisons (eg this book is heavier than that).

● It is important to recognise the two methods of comparison in frequent use: 'how much longer' (leading eventually to subtraction) and 'how many times as long' (leading to ideas of ratio and eventually to division).

- Development of appropriate language is vital at this stage and should *not* be hurried.
- Using arbitrary measures, such as parts of the body, cupfuls, pebbles, conkers etc.
- Agreeing on non-standard units, such as a cube or a drinking straw.
- The need and then the use of standard units.

All these experiences are similar for all measuring – length, weight, volume, area, time, angle and temperature. However, for some measurement, the ideas can be seen much more clearly: for example, to put four children in order of height is not too difficult for many infants, but to order just three parcels by weight presents a much more complicated problem.

- Weight or mass? Throughout the primary years the term 'weight' should be generally used. It is strictly a measure of the earth's pull on the given object. As children become more interested in the language of space travel, the more sophisticated 'mass' can be introduced. This is the term used to define the quantity of matter in a body. The mass remains constant wherever the body is, whereas the weight of a given object varies with the gravitational attraction. For example, the gravitational pull is greater on the earth than it is on the moon.
- Volume is the amount of space taken up by an object. For example, working in the classroom, a group of pupils may choose a small cube as their unit of volume. If they make a large cube from, say, eight of these basic ones, then 8 is a (non-standard) measure of its volume. At a much later stage, the standard measure of the volume of an object (the cubic metre) can be introduced.
- Capacity is simply the measure of the volume of a liquid which can be poured into a given container. The standard unit is the litre.
- Finally, the content of the curriculum must be reviewed continually in the light of technological developments, particularly in microcomputing.

Classroom approaches and assessment

These are dealt with on pages 95 and 103 but the following suggestions may bear repetition.

If you feel it is necessary to adopt a system whereby the mathematics is divided into, for example, 'first year junior work' etc, remember that in each class there will be pupils for whom the 'average' work is too easy and others for whom it is too hard. *All* pupils must be catered for. Boredom through repetition is just as harmful as confusions through misunderstanding.

Assessment should be continuous, not just an end-of-term yardstick to ascertain what is *not* known. It is a means to an end and should develop out of the aims, objectives and criteria of the curriculum. The assessment should cover not only the facts and skills but also conceptual structures and general strategies.

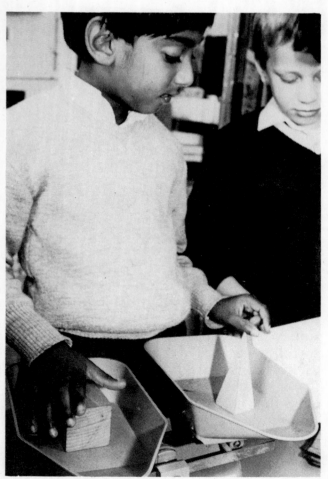

'Weight' is easier to understand than 'mass'.

Conclusions

There are many ways of teaching and learning mathematics and there is no one 'right' way.

A simple sequence for solving any mathematical problem is 'do', then 'discuss' and finally 'write'. This applies equally to a simple sum or a more complicated mathematical relationship. Naturally when the relevant facts (such as number bonds) have been well learned, the 'do' and 'discuss' stages can be dispensed with, for life at school is too short to go on discovering the wheel forever. But, from time to time, however well facts appear to be learned, it is the wise teacher who will sometimes request an explanation.

There are reasonably defined stages of progression within the topics themselves and these may be found clearly set out in the DES *Handbook of Suggestions*: *Mathematics 5–11*. They are also defined in very practical terms for infants in *Pointers* (CUP).

Finally, in spite of all the guidance available, there are many decisions to be made by each school. For example:
● What terms shall be used for 'add to' – 'plus', 'add', 'makes' etc? (Whatever decisions are made, try not to choose too many!)
● Do we teach 2-D before 3-D?
● How do we introduce the passage of time and reading the clock?
● When do we let pupils use calculators?
● Have we suitable software for microcomputing in mathematics?

● Should multiplication and division be taught concurrently or separately?
● Is there a place for first ideas of probability, logic etc?

There is no shortage of topics for debate, but above all it must always be mathematics for the children, not the children for mathematics.

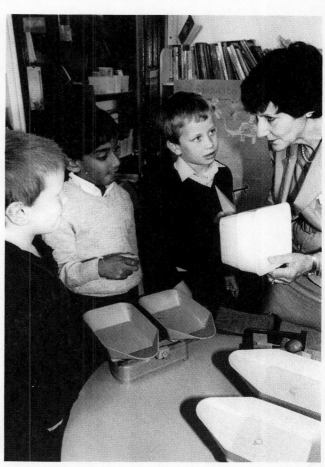

First 'do', then 'discuss', finally 'write'.

Maths within the curriculum

Maths within the curriculum

INTRODUCTION

Over the past few years mathematics schemes have flooded the market. They have helped to structure primary mathematics but in doing so they have tended to isolate mathematics from the rest of the curriculum. We would not expect children's only experience of reading to be through a reading scheme but often children's mathematical experiences rely almost exclusively on a mathematics scheme. Moreover, many mathematical opportunities within the curriculum are missed because they do not seem to be overtly mathematical: ie concerned with computation, measurement or shape.

Mathematics is much more than this.

It can be separated into two strands – utilitarian, where maths is a useful tool serving all other areas of the curriculum and everyday life, and intrinsic, interesting for its own sake. Problem solving is an example of utilitarian maths, and investigational work is often an example of the intrinsic nature of the subject. However, mathematics is not only a body of knowledge but also a process. Whenever people classify and organise information into a logical framework, they can be said to be thinking and/or acting mathematically. By adopting this wider view, many mathematical opportunities become apparent within the whole primary curriculum.

The curriculum

The curriculum can be seen as comprising nine areas of learning and experience: aesthetic and creative, human and social, linguistic and literary, mathematical, moral, physical, scientific, spiritual and technological.

These are not discrete, separate elements but are interwoven and enmeshed and should be viewed as a whole. But this is not the complete story.

In addition to the nine areas of learning and experience, the curriculum consists of the approaches used in the classroom and the elements of learning which are both interdependent. For example, exposition and practice may be used together to develop a skill. However, it is extremely unlikely that exposition alone would be an effective method to develop a concept where a range of practical experiences would be more appropriate.

Approaches

These are the styles of interaction between the teacher, the pupils and the curriculum activities. All of the approaches in the model should be used in teaching, and different tasks require different approaches.

Elements of learning

The five elements of learning are mental structures which teachers seek to develop in the children through the curriculum activities.

Facts

Facts are items of information which are unconnected and not supported by concepts. For example, notational conventions:
4^2 means 4×4

or ½ means half.

Mathematical processes can be applied across the whole of the primary curriculum.

Concepts

Concepts are ideas growing continually in the mind. They are richly interconnected making conceptual structures. In the event of a memory failure they allow us to 'build up' a route to the solution. For example:
9×9 is needed and has been forgotten
9×10 is known – 90
9×9 is one 9 less
$90 - 9 = 81$.

15

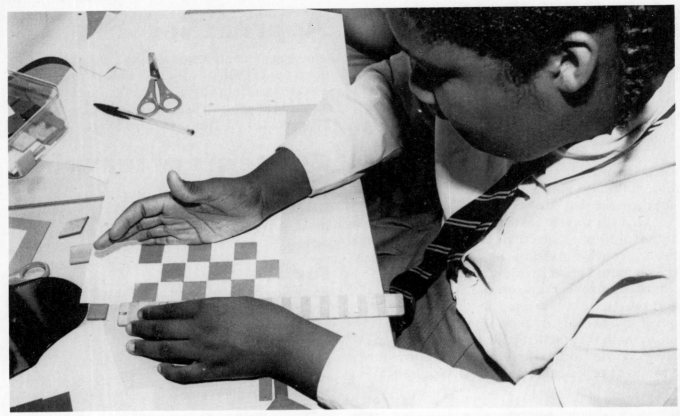

Skills, such as measuring, are one of the five elements of learning to be developed across the curriculum.

Skills

Skills are well established multi-step procedures. They can be mental or physical. For example:
- a mental skill would be an approximation or estimation etc,
- a physical skill would be using a protractor, cutting a straight line etc.

Strategies

Strategies are deciding what to do and how to do it, making choices about which skills and knowledge to use. For example, looking for pattern, making and testing hypotheses or simplifying difficult tasks.

Attitudes

Attitudes are also learned in school, and messages are conveyed in the classroom, possibly unintentionally. We all hope to engender positive attitudes towards the work, such as confidence, enjoyment and interest.

Example

Question: you spend £3.75, how much change do you get from £5?

Fact

From memory: £1.25.

Skill

By algorithm: 5.00
              −3.75
              ‾‾‾‾‾

Concept

By deduction:
£3.75 + £0.25 = £4.00
£4.00 + £1.00 = £5.00
so change is £1.00 + £0.25 = £1.25.

Strategy

By estimation, by trial and error, by simplification.

Attitude

The solver's attitude will pervade the attempted solution and probably would determine the approach used, or even whether there is any attempt made at all.

16

Objectives

The objectives for this approach do not apply to any particular area of experience and learning but rather to the elements of learning. It seems logical when adopting a cross-curricular approach to identify objectives that support the whole curriculum and not specific aspects of it.

It should:
● provide a broad balanced and relevant curriculum;
● encourage the transfer of knowledge throughout the curriculum;
● provide the children with an overall view of the curriculum, allowing concepts to be developed that do not rely on any particular subjects;
● provide more opportunities for the practice of skills in other contexts;
● encourage positive attitudes to learning and present the curriculum in a relevant and purposeful way.

Levels of development

Since this chapter develops an approach that teachers can use to analyse the curriculum, it follows that it is applicable for use with children of all ages.

Getting started

In the curriculum model, the links between the approaches, elements of learning and the areas of learning and experience were explored. Now we are going to look in more depth at the interaction between the elements of learning and the nine areas of learning and experience. If we take just one area (in this case we will use mathematics) it can be highlighted and developed through the other eight. This will be explained by the 'umbrella' model.

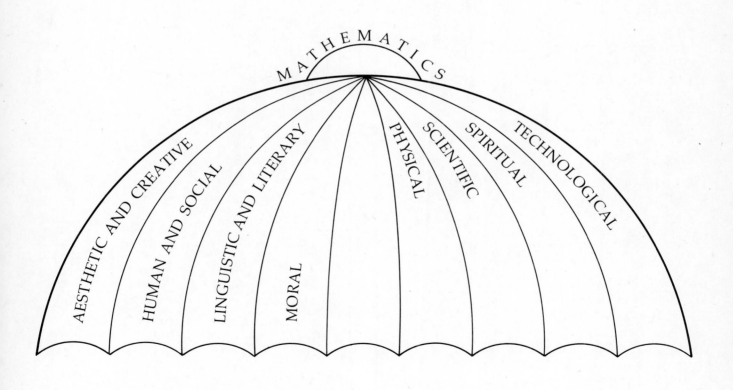

The model shows eight areas of learning and experience under the umbrella of mathematics. An element of learning (ie a fact, concept, skill, strategy or attitude) can be identified to be developed through the areas of learning and experience. In this case we have chosen the concept of 'pattern'. It would have been equally possible to have chosen a skill (eg listening), or an attitude (eg caring), or a strategy (eg trial and error). It would also have been possible to have identified a fact but since facts are isolated bodies of knowledge they would prove to be much less fruitful in terms of learning than one of the other four elements.

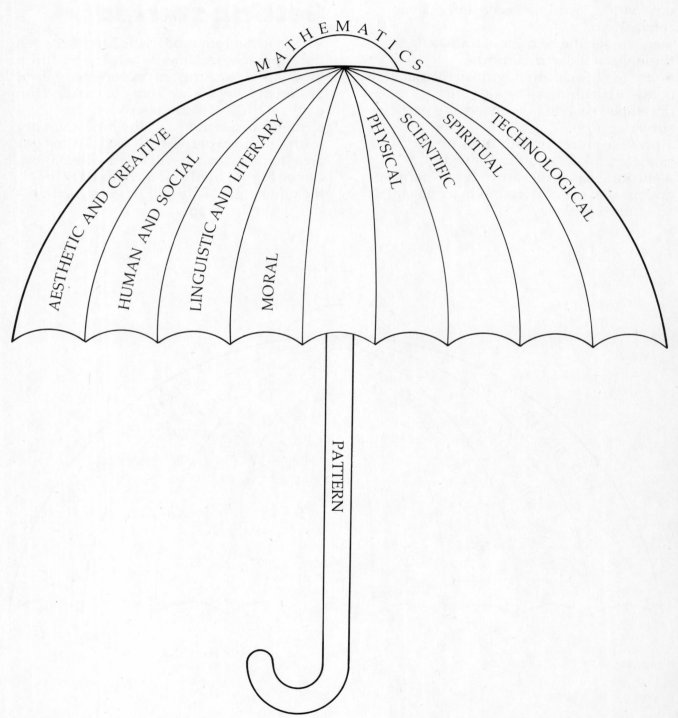

The concept of 'pattern' forms the handle of the umbrella and is the basis for further analysis. Tasks can be identified from each of the eight segments of the umbrella, bearing in mind the fundamental concept of pattern and the overall area of mathematics. In the model these are identified by raindrops.

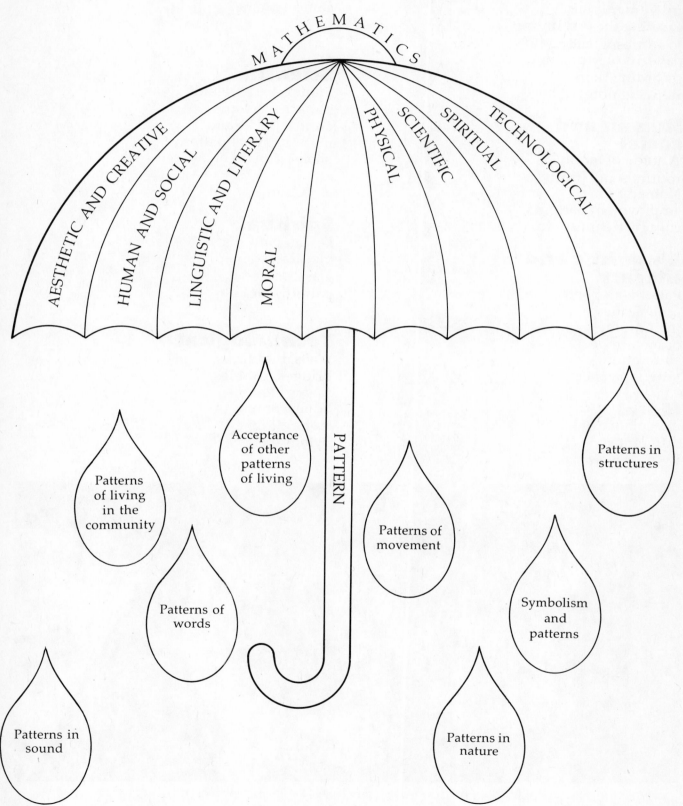

MATHEMATICS

AESTHETIC AND CREATIVE

HUMAN AND SOCIAL

LINGUISTIC AND LITERARY

MORAL

PHYSICAL

SCIENTIFIC

SPIRITUAL

TECHNOLOGICAL

PATTERN

Patterns of living in the community

Acceptance of other patterns of living

Patterns of words

Patterns of movement

Patterns in structures

Symbolism and patterns

Patterns in sound

Patterns in nature

Aesthetic and creative

Creating patterns of sound using the body, home-made musical instruments etc. Relating these sounds to stories. Creating patterns of sound and recording them, noticing note values.

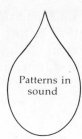

Patterns in sound

Human and social

A study of family routines and lifestyles. Noticing time, employment patterns, cultural richness etc.

Patterns of living in the community

Linguistic and literary

Patterns in poetry, mnemonics, palindromes, onomatopoeia, alliteration, tongue twisters.

Patterns of words

Moral

Acceptance of different styles of living. Tolerance.

Acceptance of other patterns of living

Physical

Routes, directions, angles.
Repeated patterns.
Methodical actions.
Dance, drama.

Patterns of movement

Scientific

Honeycombs, cloud patterns, crystals, animal tracks and markings, leaf patterns, shells, growth etc.

Patterns in nature

Spiritual

Diwali patterns, mosaics, stained glass, seasonal patterns etc.

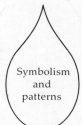

Symbolism and patterns

Technological

Walls, buildings, bridges, cobbles, tower blocks, honeycombs, scaffolding, pylons etc.

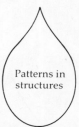

Patterns in structures

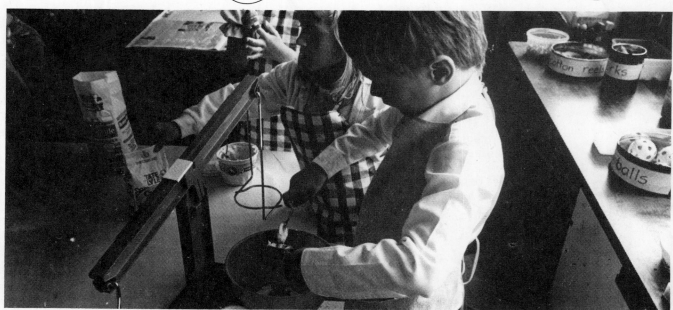

Cooking is fun, and it enables children to practise mathematical skills such as weighing and timing.

This model is useful in curriculum planning throughout the school. However, it deals with the topics in a very general way. For the individual class teacher, further analysis of a more short-term nature will be necessary. Attention will need to be focused on each particular raindrop and possible tasks identified.

Another way is to analyse the elements of learning that would be developed through a task. The example shows how the activity of cooking is a particularly fruitful cross-curricular activity.

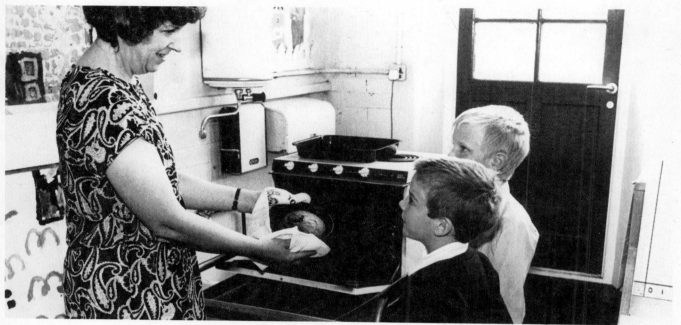

Once the cake is cooked, the concept of sharing and fractions can be introduced or practised.

Cooking

Aesthetic and creative
Act of creation, decoration, awareness of degrees of quality.

Human and social
Agriculture.
Industrial catering.
Shopping.
Regional variations.
National variations.

Linguistic and literary
Language from experience.
Listening and talking.
Technical language.
Follow written or spoken instructions.

Scientific
Decay.
Observing.
Experimenting.

Applying knowledge to new situations.
Organise and select from observations.

Mathematical
Comparing.
One-to-one correspondence.
Ordering.
Weighing.
Sharing.
Time.
Ratio.

Moral
Acceptance of dietary variations.
Co-operation.
Use of resources.
Consider consequences of own actions.
Make informed choices.
Sharing.

Physical
Motor skills.
Health issues.

Technological
Planning.
Making to standards.
Evaluating.
Using and adapting tools.

Both these models are ways of assisting in the analysis of cross-curricular study. It is important to look closely at what you are doing in school, so that you are able to justify this work fully in times when outside agencies are becoming more deeply involved in the educational debate. One thing that you can be sure of, however, is that you will meet at least two of the criteria for the curriculum in the policy statement *Better Schools* – that the curriculum is broad and balanced.

Follow-up
Follow-up from these activities is preferably derived from spontaneous questions from the children or particular interests that they may show. This capitalises on the children as a learning resource, an idea which will be more fully explored in the next chapter.

Children as investigators

Children as investigators

INTRODUCTION

Historically society has held a narrow view of mathematics, concentrating almost solely on the four rules of number. The Cockcroft Report, however, strongly advocates an investigative approach which will lead children into becoming mathematical thinkers, not simply rule followers. By stimulating questioning and allowing children to wonder 'What happens if . . .?' they will be better prepared for dealing with the various ways in which mathematics can be used in life.

The teacher, using the professional skills of questioning, creating a particular learning environment, and knowing when to stand back, is a powerful resource. The child also brings to the learning situation an accumulation of past experience, and interaction with the environment motivates the child to enquire further. It is wasteful to ignore the potential of the child as a learning resource. Children are active learners and mathematics is an active process. Learning is more permanent and well rooted if children actually participate in mathematics themselves rather than attempting to absorb the body of mathematical knowledge passively.

This chapter provides a number of starting points which could be used to give children opportunities to explore mathematical possibilities. One particular example is illustrated in some depth to indicate the breadth of children's potential as mathematical thinkers.

Objectives

The main reasons for using the investigative approach are:
- to increase children's confidence in order that they may be personally involved in their own mathematical learning;
- to extend children's mathematical thinking;
- to extend the range of mathematical strategies available to children: eg trial and error, simplifying the problem and looking for pattern;
- to encourage children to follow logical deductive processes.

A simple game prompts the investigation of shapes.

Level of development

The open-ended nature of an investigative approach is such that the actual topic to be investigated can often be presented to children of varying levels of development. The children will approach the problem at their own level of ability and the end result tends to reflect each child's particular strengths.

Classroom organisation

Setting up resources

A range of resources should be available in the classroom, stored so that they are clearly visible and attractively presented. Children should make their own decisions as to which resources would best meet their needs, and should know where to find them.

These materials need not be expensive and can include junk materials, various types of paper and card, collections of natural objects, and so on. Whatever the resources are, it is essential that children of all stages of development are allowed plenty of opportunities to explore the materials fully in their own way. This will allow them to begin to understand the properties of the equipment, and by discussion they can start to refine their thoughts. Some useful photocopiable sheets are given on pages 126 to 128.

Classroom resources may include junk materials.

Ideally, investigative work should arise from questions posed by the children; however, it is often prudent to have a bank of starting points available in the classroom. Some ideas for these are presented later in the chapter.

Grouping

The investigative approach allows opportunities for children to work individually, pursuing ideas in an area of particular interest to them, often in the child's own time following on from a school-initiated activity.

However, a more common arrangement is for the children to work co-operatively in small groups. These groups can be either teacher-organised, in which case it is important that multiracial and gender issues are borne in mind, or chosen by the children, who then take responsibility for deciding the size and composition of their working group.

In response to a child's question it may be appropriate to involve the whole class in the investigative process. Although the class involvement is likely to be of short duration, such discussion can often prove to be the starting point for an individual or group activity.

Investigations encourage children to work in groups, discussing and working co-operatively.

Posing questions

The investigative approach relies on the asking of questions. Children should be involved in their own learning, posing and resolving their own enquiries. Traditionally the teaching of mathematics has tended to depend on the transmission of skills, and children have been discouraged from thinking and being responsible for their own learning. By transforming children's statements into questions, teachers can encourage them to become mathematical thinkers. For example, the statement 'All odd numbers are prime' is commonly heard in the classroom. It can be adapted to become 'Is there an odd number that is not prime?' providing an opportunity for mathematical enquiry.

One method of encouraging children to be mathematical investigators is for the teacher to pose open-ended questions. For example:

● How do you know?
● Is there another way?
● How can you be sure?
● Why do you think this happens?
● Is this always the case?
● Where can you find another example?

Prompt investigation by asking questions.

Investigating flags

The following example illustrates how the same investigative starting point has been tackled by teachers of children throughout the primary age range:

When tried out in schools it has led to

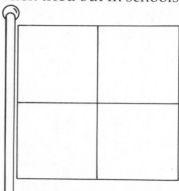

Find as many flags as possible using two colours.

● What happens if . . .?

As children become more used to this approach they begin to pose their own questions more frequently.

many colourful displays and much considered enquiry by the children. Photocopiable sheets for flags are given on pages 129 to 134.

An investigation into flags divided into four squares was adapted for every primary age group.

Five- to seven-year-olds

Two different starting points were used

with this age group. In the first, the children started by folding squares of paper once then twice, and discussing the number of sections created. The idea of colouring the sections was then used. The second

29

introduction used four interlocking squares which were arranged in as many ways as possible. Discussion centred on which of these arrangements was the most suitable to make a flag.

Arrangements of four squares

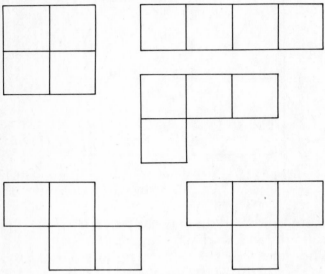

The children organised their own working groups depending on which arrangement they had chosen to use. They explored ways of creating patterns with only two colours of square. Discussion centred around whether the patterns were the same or different from those that had already been found. The children discovered that if the patterns were rotated there were only four different ones. The idea of a flag with a flagpole was then introduced, making rotation impossible, and the children then set about finding as many flags as possible.

Allowing rotations

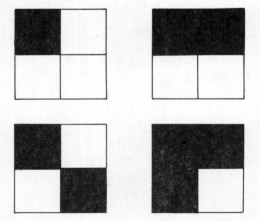

The idea of grouping the flags was then introduced, leading to the children identifying sets. It was clear that they benefited from discussing the reasons behind their classification. One popular grouping was:

Set 1

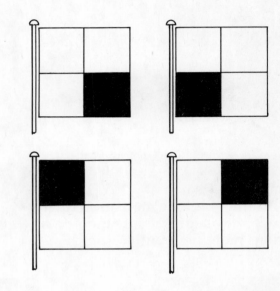

Set 2

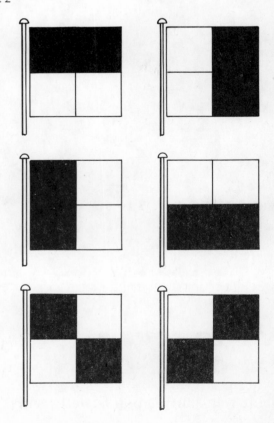

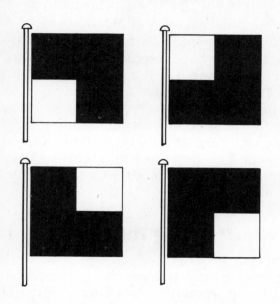

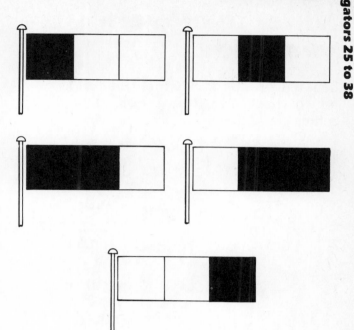

Classifying in this way helped the children to identify flags that they may have missed.

A further extension of this was to paint the flags. One child suggested that paint could be mixed in the ratios 1:3, 2:2 and 3:1 as they had grouped the flags. These colour tones were then used to paint the children's own designs.

Seven- to nine-year-olds

For this age group the task was introduced by first of all dealing with two squares and two colours.

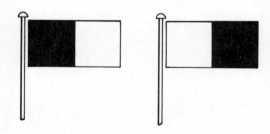

This was extended to three squares by the children in response to the question 'What would happen if . . .?'.

Extending it further to four squares, two arrangements were considered: ie four in a row and four in a square. The flags were then grouped by the children, who began to identify their own questions and divided into groups accordingly. One group looked at using a different number of colours, another at different arrangements of squares. Yet another looked at how many patterns could be found if rotations were deemed to be the same. A more adventurous group looked at international flags and investigated their patterns.

Children studied the possible colour combinations.

31

Nine- to eleven-year-olds

This age group quickly identified a logical way of discovering the number of flags which could be made.

I first looked at all the flags with one red square. Then I found the two's and the three's. I noticed the three's were the same as the one's.

They went on to investigate different numbers of squares and began to look for a pattern in the number of flags they could make. One group preferred to investigate ways of splitting a square into quarters and through this work they began to focus on the properties of a quarter. Another group chose to explore dividing a square into four sections and colouring using only two colours. They discovered many designs and concluded that they could have gone on for ever!

Starting points

The previous example showed how one starting point could be used across the entire primary age range. This section provides some starting points for investigation work that are based on two mathematical themes. One is numerical and the other is spatial. These ideas are purely beginnings and should be further developed with the children through their own interests or through the questioning technique.

Investigating five

A Socks
Investigate how many socks you need to pull out of a drawer to ensure you have a matching pair. (You have four colours of socks: red, yellow, green and blue).

B Five in nature
Investigate patterns of five in nature eg starfish, horse-chestnut leaves etc.

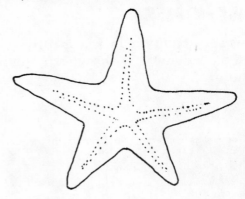

C Five digits
Investigate different ways of arranging five different digits.

D Patterns of five

Investigate patterns of five using four different coloured counters (eg yellow, blue, red, green, green, or red, yellow, blue, green, red).

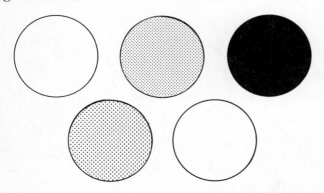

E Alphabet

Investigate the nodes of the letters of the alphabet. Are there any with five nodes? Why?

F Five-sided polygons

Investigate different ways of cutting out five-sided shapes.

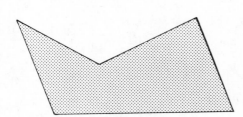

G Five bridges

Investigate ways of crossing the river.

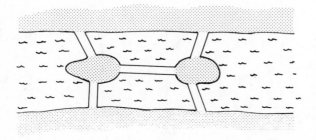

H Greetings cards

Investigate five friends sending cards to each other.

I Grids

Investigate placing five counters on a 3 × 3 grid.

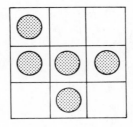

J Wolves and lambs

Investigate how two wolves and three lambs could cross a river using one boat that only holds two animals. If the wolves ever outnumber the lambs, they eat them.

K Five cubes

Investigating the arrangements that can be made using five linking cubes.

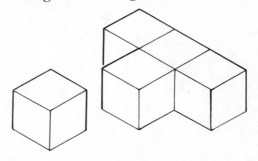

33

L Five dice
Investigate throwing five dice.

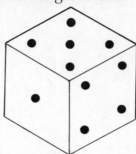

M Five shapes to make a solid
Investigate making solid shapes using linking triangles and squares.

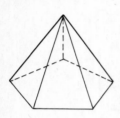
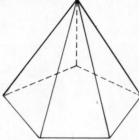

N Frogs
Investigate four frogs crossing a pond

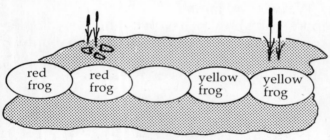

The frogs should exchange sides. They can only move forwards by sliding one space or hopping over one other frog.

O Five letters in my name
Investigate names containing five letters.

P Handshakes
Investigate a group of five people shaking hands with each other.

Q Making five
Investigate ways of adding numbers to make five.

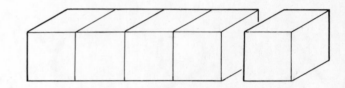

R Five dots
Investigate ways of joining five dots on dotted paper.

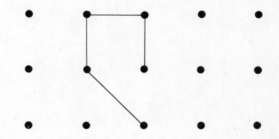

S Symbols for five
Investigate ways of representing five.

Children tried a series of activities which involved the investigation of the number five.

Investigating cubes

A Staircase
Investigate staircases built with cubes.

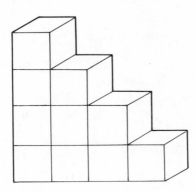

B Nets
Investigate the nets of cubes.

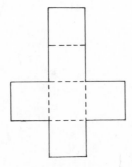

C Paint the face
Investigate cubes with faces painted different colours.

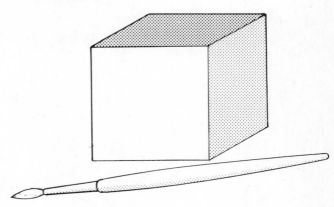

D Cubes around us
Investigate cubes in the environment eg crystals, buildings etc.

35

E Creating dice
Investigate different numbers on dice.

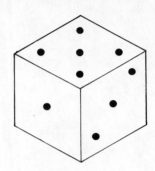

F Stacking dice
Investigate dice in stacks.

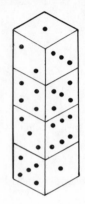

G Isometric cubes
Investigate patterns of isometric cubes (use photocopiable resource sheet on page 135).

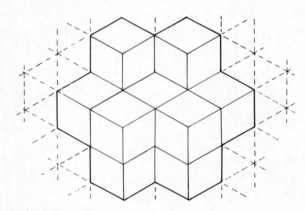

H Drawing cubes
Investigate drawing cubes (using various techniques including isometric drawing).

I Cube shadows
Investigate shadows made by one or more cube.

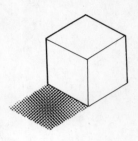

J Mirror cubes
Investigate cubes reflected in two angled mirrors.

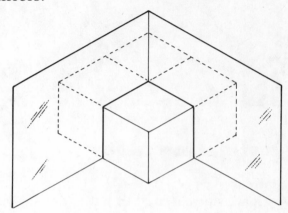

K Pyramid cubes
Investigate pyramids built with cubes.

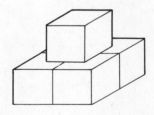

L Hollow cubes
Investigate hollow cubes built with interlocking cubes.

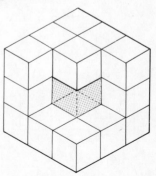

M Cutting cubes
Investigate cutting cubes made of modelling material or polystyrene.

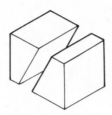

N Towers of cubes
Investigate the patterns in four towers of four cubes each using only two colours.

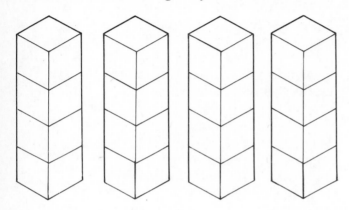

O Hidden cubes
Investigate hidden cubes in structures built with interlocking cubes.

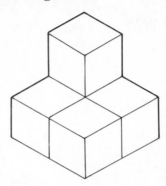

P Enlarging cubes
Investigate the effect on the volume of a cube when the length of the side is increased.

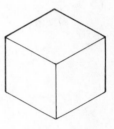

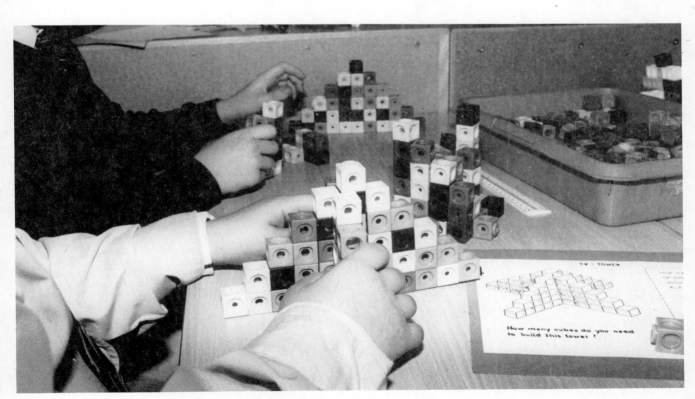

Encourage children to pursue their investigation from a given starting point, such as building pyramids.

Follow-up

A stimulating mathematical environment can be created by making a display of objects and children's work that promotes enquiry.

- Things to look at:
  – children's work
  – kaleidoscopes

Objects like this kaleidoscope on display in the classroom will stimulate questioning and investigation.

  – magnifying glasses
  – photographs
  – patterns etc

- Things to listen to:
  – shells
  – tape recordings
  – musical boxes
  – things to rattle
  – clocks etc

- Things to feel:
  – textured materials
  – feely boxes/bags
  – natural objects
  – solid shapes
  – textured numerals etc

- Things to taste and smell:
  – containers that are now empty eg spice, soap, perfume containers
  – herbs
  – flowers
  – selection of white powders to identify eg flour, sugar, salt etc
  – liquids

- Things to talk about:
  – games and puzzles
  – photographs from odd angles
  – things to construct
  – mirrors
  – slides etc

- Things to think about
  – books, newspapers and magazine articles
  – computer activities
  – calculators
  – statistical information
  – brain teasers etc

Creating a provoking environment and encouraging questioning will help children to show that they are active mathematical thinkers, always wondering what would happen if . . .?

Developing problem solving

Developing problem solving

INTRODUCTION

As is pointed out in *Mathematics 5-16*, there are often unpleasant connotations in the word 'problem'. The ability to solve problems, however, is at the heart of mathematics. This leaves all who are concerned with mathematics education with a serious dilemma because these unpleasant connotations are brought by the children into school. The teacher's problem is to overcome the negative feelings of children towards the subject. Using a more enquiry-based approach is one way to help children increase in confidence and allow them to relax enough to begin to enjoy mathematics.

The word 'problem' in mathematical terms means that there is a situation that needs to be solved, either one which has arisen naturally or one which has been set up especially. Roy Hollands defines a 'problem' as 'a task requiring reasoning and not capable of being done by remembered technique alone . . . that is, a problem for one person is not necessarily a problem for another'. A simple computation sum such as 5×3 is unlikely to be a problem but 'How much are three sweets at five pence each?' may be a problem if the pupils do not know which operation to use.

There are five categories of mathematical problem encountered by children in primary schools: abstract, contextual, tangible, realistic and real.

Abstract

Problems in this category are likely to be of a purely mathematical nature. For example, children may be asked to find the area of a hexagon without being given a prescribed technique for doing so. Various materials such as squared paper, scissors etc, should be available. When tackling this problem several workable solutions will emerge, encouraging the children to seek others.

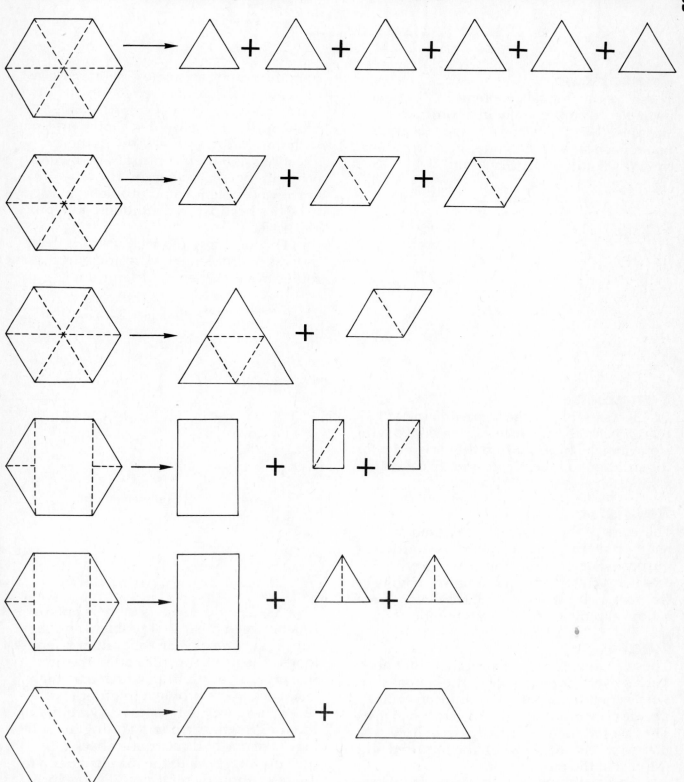

Contextual

These are theoretical problems which have been placed superficially in a context. For example: 'Mrs Jones has a hexagonal garden pond. Each side of the pond measures 100 cm. What is the area of the pond?'

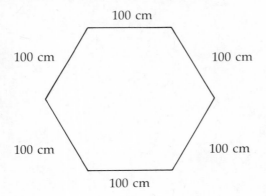

Tangible

Problems in this category are illustrated by real objects. For instance a hexagonal paving stone may be brought into the classroom for the children to investigate and discover its area.

Realistic

These are problems which are based on reality but are being solved for no particular purpose. For example, the area of a school courtyard covered with hexagonal paving stones may be investigated. However, there is no real purpose to discovering the area.

Real

These problems are real problems that need to be solved. For example, if the school wishes to build a path, the children could decide on what shape paving stones to use. They would then need to discover how many paving stones would be required and the cost of the job.

The first three categories are classroom-based activities that may have originated from the school's scheme of work. The last two categories are an application of mathematics in the real world. Ideally problem-solving activities should originate with the children, arising out of their questions and their concerns and be firmly based in the 'real' category. However, this is not always practical and problems may have to be teacher-inspired although preferably still 'real'.

The following model illustrates the process of problem-solving and analyses the routes from problem to resolution.

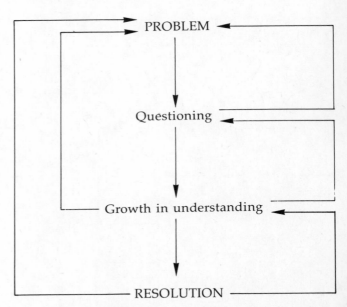

As the model shows there is not a direct link between the initial problem and the subsequent resolution, but rather a series of loops. The problem will lead in the first instance to questioning which may then lead back to the problem in order to re-examine it or to reassess its viability. From a growth in understanding the solver may take one of three routes; back to questioning, back to the problem or on to the resolution. Several circuits may have to be made before the resolution can be reached. Indeed, after accepting the resolution the solver may re-examine the problem yet again, in order to assess the practicality of the resolution or to check its applicability to other similar problems.

Objectives

The objectives of a problem-solving approach are both wide-ranging and cross-curricular. The most important ones are as follows:
● to present children with learning situations that are enjoyable, purposeful and relevant;
● to encourage children to adopt a more enquiring approach to their learning;
● to encourage children to become actively involved in organising their own learning;
● to give children opportunities to organise their own problem solving strategies;
● to encourage children to become more self-reliant and resourceful;
● to provide opportunities for experimentation in mathematics.

Children must be familiar with all the maths resources.

All problems will provide opportunities for children to develop and increase the strategies available to them and to approach the task in a logical fashion. Strategic and logical thought are the foundation of all mathematics and their importance should not be underestimated.

Level of development

Most real problem-solving activities can be tackled by children of every level of development. Their approaches to the problem and their strategies for solving it will differ and will be dependent on their intellectual maturity. If the problem is one that has been identified by the children themselves it is likely to be appropriate to their level of development. Children gain most by tackling problems which are just within their capabilities.

Classroom organisation

It would be unrealistic to discuss only real problem solving activities. Asking children to be responsible for their own learning in a situation where the solution is vital can be a daunting prospect for all concerned, both teachers and children. Children need to have had experience of organising their own learning and developing their own strategies as well as being familiar with all the mathematical resources available. This experience can be provided by smaller 'on-the-spot' problems that can be easily adapted from standard tasks in mathematics schemes or books. For instance, a task often seen in infant workbooks is:

1	2	☐	4	☐
☐	7	☐	☐	10

fill in the missing numbers

This can be adapted to sorting a pack of cards to discover if there are any missing. Many different strategies can be used to approach this latter problem whereas the earlier task is very restricting.

An example from a book for seven-year-olds could be:

What is the time?
Write down the time in figures and words under each clock.
The second one has been done for you.

A

....

....

1.15
....
one fifteen
....

....

....

....

....

This task could be adapted to working out a rota for when children can visit the school library.

A task commonly featuring in books for nine-year-olds and upwards is:

$$£$$
$$1.49$$
$$\times\ 13$$

———

———

A more fruitful and relevant task might be to check how much dinner money had been collected and compare that total with how much should have been collected.

These 'on-the-spot' problems can occur on an everyday basis and will encourage the children to think of their own examples. On the other hand the more extended problems will probably be undertaken on a termly basis at best. They only successfully occur when the children are comfortable in and familiar with their classroom environment. Providing a well equipped mathematical resource area that is freely available to the children to make their own choices is essential.

Teacher's strategies

These can be divided into those concerned with giving security and those concerned with enabling learning.

Probably the most important strategy in the first group is listening. As teachers will know, it is very difficult to resist the temptation to talk when we should listen.

ANDRÉ COLLETT

Listening is important for providing security.

46

Other strategies include appreciating children's efforts, however minimal, understanding that there are many different routes to a solution and accepting all workable solutions. Try not to hold preconceived notions of the 'perfect' or conventional solution or the 'correct' method.

The second group of strategies enable children to learn from their problem-solving activities. The foremost of these is to ask yourself continually 'Who's doing the thinking here?' The skill of questioning as detailed in the chapter on 'Children as investigators' (see page 25) is also very important to problem-solving.

Whilst solving problems, children may come across the need to use certain mathematics that they have not previously encountered. It is quite appropriate at these times for the class teacher to interrupt the activity to teach what is needed. A skill that has been taught at the point it is needed by the children will be much more easily learned.

Children's strategies

In the initial stages of problem-solving strategies that predominate include observation, classification, brainstorming and reflection. Children will also need to begin to organise their thoughts, the tasks and themselves, and it is important that they look at the constraints of the situation in which they are working.

As the work progresses other strategies come to the forefront. They include questioning, hypothesising, using resources imaginatively, trial and error, and reasoning.

Attention should also be given to recording information and communicating the solution to others either in written or verbal form. It is important that children can clearly state their case verbally in order to be able to justify their solution to the teacher or their peers. Verbalisation clarifies thought and is a useful device to ensure that what they have done has been clearly understood.

Throughout the stages of problem solving, children should be encouraged to

Children must be able to explain and justify their solution to their peers to clarify their own thoughts.

think about the following questions.
- What are we working towards?
- What are the constraints?
- Are there other considerations to be taken into account?
- How should we organise ourselves?
- What resources do we need?
- Is what we are doing achievable?

It is essential that the solution arrived at by the children is put into effect and that they can see the final result of their work. Otherwise the problem solving is reduced to a pointless activity in their eyes. The solution is unlikely to be purely mathematical but a tremendous amount of mathematical thinking will have gone into its discovery.

Example

This problem-solving exercise will strike a chord in many teachers' hearts – the perennial problem of the cloakroom. Not enough space! Not enough pegs! Where do we put the lunch boxes? Can we reach the shoe bags? Coats on the floor! Wellingtons! Wet coats! etc

Space in the cloakroom posed a real problem.

Although this particular case worked with six- and seven-year-olds, it could be tackled successfully by children across the primary age range.

Stage 1: discussion
The class spent some time discussing the nature of the problem and all the things about their cloakroom which they did not like or were unsuccessful and concerned them. The whole class was involved as they all had their own particular grievances.

Stage 2: suggested solutions
All suggested solutions were considered by the class. Some were thought to be unworkable so the children sorted them into two groups: 'possible' and 'impossible'. Justification had to be given for the classification. For example, the suggestion that a new larger cloakroom be built was thought to be impractical because of the cost.

Stage 3: trialling
All the possible solutions were then trialled, each solution being given a week to operate. The appropriateness of each solution was then discussed and the two best were chosen.

Stage 4: modification
The two chosen solutions were modified in the light of the experience of the week's trial and certain elements of rejected solutions were incorporated. For example, a one-way system of movement had been rejected but a limited one-way system at certain times of the day was incorporated into one of the two best solutions.

Stage 5: retrialling
Each of the two solutions was then retrialled for a longer period.

Stage 6: selection
The final chosen solution was arrived at by a democratic process involving voting.

Stage 7: adaptation
The chosen solution was then applied to other forms of organisation in the classroom.

Starting points

Problems that arise from the children are most likely to have links with the school as in the previous example. The following diagram shows some ideas for starting points in and around the school. Ultimately problems should be those perceived by the children as their own. However, in the meantime problems will need to be, at least to some extent, teacher-inspired. By the teacher asking questions rather than directing, the children will be provoked into problem-solving activities and encouraged to ask their own questions.

The ideas in the diagram are all based on the school and are further sub-divided into three categories: everyday, environmental and events.

The environment provides a variety of problems to solve.

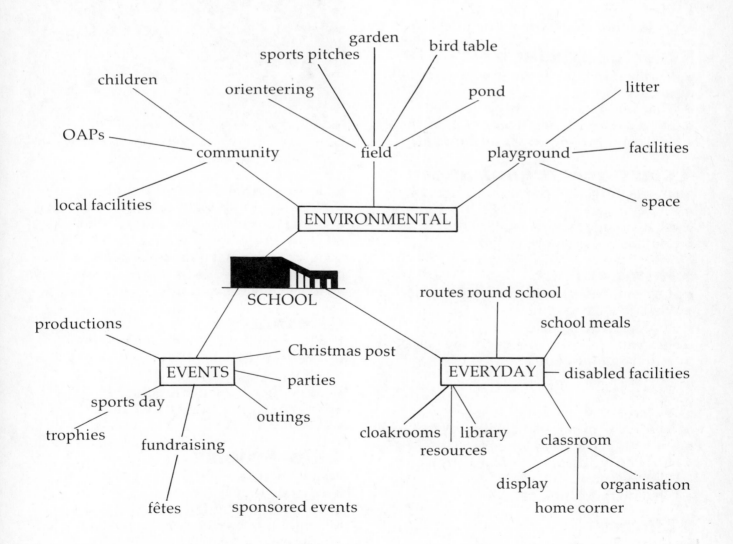

Everyday

1 Routes around school
- How many routes are there around school?
- Which are the best?
- Are they clearly signposted?
- Are there some doors that are hardly used?
- Are there some routes that can only be used when it's not raining?
- What routes should be used if there was a fire?

2 School meals
- How many children have school meals?
- Why do some children have sandwiches?
- What types of food are best to eat?
- What types of food are most popular?
- What would be a good menu?
- Could lunch be served more quickly?

3 Disabled facilities
- What facilities are there in school for the disabled?
- What facilities do the disabled need?
- Could a wheelchair get around the school?
- How could we improve the situation?

4 Classroom organisation
- How is the classroom organised now?
- What things are necessary in the room?
- What storage facilities are there?
- Could it be better organised?

5 Home corner
- How can we look after the home corner?
- What do we need in it?
- How can we organise it?
- How can we make sure everyone has a fair turn in the home corner?

6 Display
- What display space have we got?
- What work do we usually display?
- Can we get different types of work?
- How can we display it to best effect?
- Who sees our display?
- What do they think of it?

7 Library
- How is the library organised?

Could your library be better organised?

- How much shelf space is there?
- What types of books are there?
- What types of books would we like?
- Could it be better organised?
- How can we make sure every class gets a fair chance to use the library?
- How can we keep it tidy?

8 Resources
- What resources do we have in school?
- Where are they kept?
- Who uses the resources?
- Could they be better organised?
- What other resources do we need?
- How can we get them?

9 Cloakrooms
- How many people use the cloakroom?
- What do they leave there?
- Are there enough pegs?
- Could the cloakroom be better organised?
- How can we keep it tidy?

Environmental

The playground

1 Litter

- How much litter collects in the playground?
- Where does it come from?
- How can it be stopped/reduced?
- Why shouldn't litter be dropped?
- Which types of litter are biodegradable and which are not?
- How much rubbish is produced by the neighbourhood?
- What are the best methods of disposing of rubbish?
- Are there different methods for different types?
- Can some rubbish be recycled?

2 Facilities (markings etc)

- What facilities are in the playground?
- Are they suitable?
- What activities go on in the playground?
- What types of facility would be most appreciated?
- How can we change the playground?

3 Space

- How much space is there in the playground?
- Is this enough?
- Who uses the playground?
- What for?
- How can the use of the playground be better organised?
- What else could it be used for?

The field

1 Orienteering

- Would an orienteering course be appreciated?
- Who would use it?
- How long should it be?
- Where are the best places for stops?
- What type of map should be used?
- What would be the best type of directions to use?

2 Sports pitches

- What sports pitches do we have?
- What size does each type of pitch need to be?

Children could examine the playground facilities and how they are organised.

Street safety is a real problem for children, presenting a number of important questions.

- Are there some areas of the field that are unsuitable for some sports?
- How many pitches of each type do we need?
- Could we arrange the pitches to provide a more convenient layout?

3 Garden
- What type of garden do we need?
- How much space is available?
- Do we want a wild area?
- If so, what type of plants and environment would be best?
- Who is going to look after it?

4 Bird table
- What is the best type of table to use?
- How can we build a bird table?
- What materials do we need?
- Where would it be best to site a bird table?
- What type of bird is likely to use it?
- What types of food do they like?

5 Pond
- What type of pond do we want?
- Where are we going to put it?
- How can we build it?
- What materials do we need?
- What type of plants should we have?

- What animals will live in our pond?
- How can we look after it?

The community

1 Children
- How can we help younger children?
- What is there for them to do?
- How can they be kept safe?
- How many children are there in the neighbourhood?
- Can we do something for them?

2 OAPs
- What are the problems of being an OAP?
- What is there for them to do?
- What do they enjoy doing?
- How can we help?
- How can we contact them?
- How can they help us?

3 Local faciltiies
- What facilities are there locally?
- What facilities are needed?
- Why are the facilities sited where they are?
- Are there any under threat of closure?
- Does this matter?
- Who uses the facilities?

Events

1 Christmas post
- Who would use a school Christmas post?
- When should it begin?
- Where should the post box be located?
- How can the cards be delivered?

2 Parties
- What type of party?
- When should it be?
- How long should it be?
- Which games should we have?
- How can we organise the food?
- Who will help us?

3 Outings
- Where should we go?
- How can we get there?
- How much will it cost?
- Who will come?
- How long should we be away from school?
- What can we do when we get there?

4 Sponsored events
- What type of event?
- Who will take part?
- How can it be organised?
- Where will the money go?

5 Fête
- How many stalls?
- What type of stalls?
- Where can they be put?
- What day?
- How can the money be collected?
- What will the money be used for?

6 Sports day
- When should we hold it?
- What races should we have?
- Refreshments?
- What equipment will be needed?
- How can we organise the scoring of points?
- What if it rains?
- What if there's an injury?

8 Trophies
- What trophies do we need?
- How can they be made?
- What materials do we need?
- What design?

9 Productions
- What type of production should we put on?
- Who will take part?
- Who will come?
- What type of programme?
- Do we charge for tickets?
- How can we arrange the hall?
- Are there some people we should especially invite?

A school production will raise a number of questions and problems to solve.

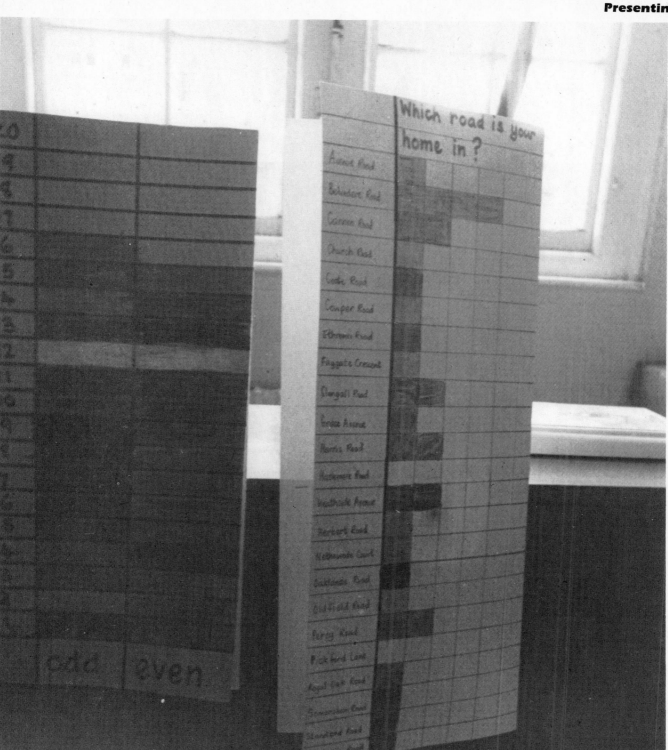

Presenting results

Presenting results

INTRODUCTION

The presentation of results is the final stage of a chain of events initiated by an idea, discussion, prepared material, a real-life situation, or any combination of these.

The teacher may know where the chain leads, in which case she can guide the children's activities, being aware in advance of the format and possibilities for recording and visual presentation. On the other hand, the teacher may explore the situation with her class, expecting them to make real decisions about possible paths to take.

In the latter case, format and type of presentation cannot be anticipated; the class must have a wealth of presentation skills to call upon.

Most classrooms will operate within these two poles. The teacher will have some expectations of the course of events, but will realise that her children may sidetrack, cul-de-sac and develop the starter themselves. Her roles will span intervention, guidance, observation, suggestion, interaction, direction and the ability to sanction mistakes. Other constraints which may occur will be a function of the children's skill level, knowledge and range of recording skills: eg the techniques needed for constructing pie charts, block graphs, scattergrams etc.

When a group of children were collecting data for a pie chart on crisp preferences, they were not happy with their class size of 27 because 'it doesn't divide easily into 360'. So they decided to obtain further data from three children from another class in order to up their divisor by three.

Displayed work can itself be a starting point: ie the presentation of results is both an end and a beginning. During the active stages of a piece of work, there is a fluidity: children may alter or amend their plans or change them completely. This interim stage can involve discussion among themselves or with their teacher, to clarify their ideas and reinforce verbal and written communication skills.

The final stage implies permanency. The immediacy takes a more rigid shape, and children explore the value of their experiences, turning them into paper presentations, such as graphs or diagrams.

Presenting results, then, is an essential part of problem-solving and investigation. It requires assessment, discussion, insight, communication, reflection and understanding. By viewing their results

objectively, they learn to empathise with an 'outsider's' view: ie to see through the eyes of a non-participant.

The final display is mainly for the children. It is of immense satisfaction to them to be appreciated by their peers, parents and teachers. But the benefits gained by adults are merely by-products; the main purpose of recording is that it benefits the children themselves.

In this chapter, three different maths projects are discussed to illustrate the type of work that is possible. They range from the cross-curricular, to a 'straight' maths problem, to one based on a real-life situation. They also vary in the extent to which they are teacher-initiated and directed.

Cross-curricular project

A story written by Nicola called 'Arthur's Zoo' was used as a starting point. In the story, five imaginary animals called Hoskins come to live at the zoo. The story introduces many mathematical ideas: the characters in the story design the zoo, draw floor plans, use grids etc.

VIVIENNE JAHANS

Children transfer their work on to paper in the final stages, as graphs, pie charts and so on.

This activity was teacher-initiated and guided, but allowed scope for creative child-directed investigations. Many aspects of the curriculum were incorporated into the project, ranging from creative writing to problem-solving.

The children were introduced to the story by being asked to design an imaginary animal that was a cross between two real animals: eg an eleswan is a cross between an elephant and a swan. They then read the story and after discussions worked either independently or in groups on the following activities over a two-day period.

Designing an animal

They were asked to decide on measurements for their animal and to design its habitat.

Designing letters

The children wrote letters to the Hoskins at the zoo and also to other Hoskins around the world, inviting them to come and live with them. This involved designing their own stamps. Also, questionnaires were designed to determine what each Hoskin liked in the way of food, accommodation etc.

Designing the zoo

This involved conservation of area. The children had to rearrange the cages and look at scale drawings. They drew some actual-size cages in the playground to determine the amount of space they had.

Attributes

The children wrote and drew about what attributes each Hoskin might have.

Plans

They worked on plans for the Hoskins' house, and compiled inventories of what would be required.

Solving the grid problem

The grid area of the house is five by five. The children had to work out how to fit the five Hoskins into it so that there would not be more than one Hoskin in any row or column. One child commented: 'The grids taught me a lot of maths. I found out that the rules don't work for a two-by-two grid.'

'This was brilliant. I liked designing the stamps and fitting them to the envelopes.' Scott

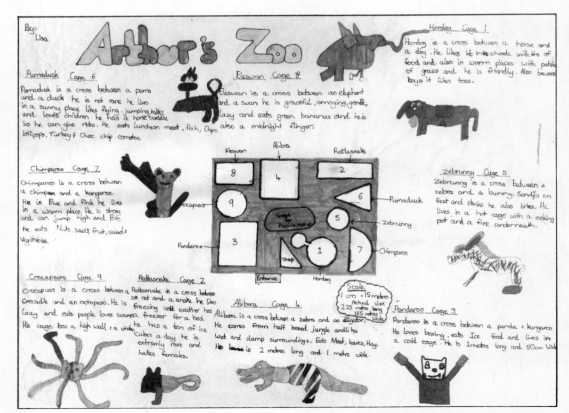

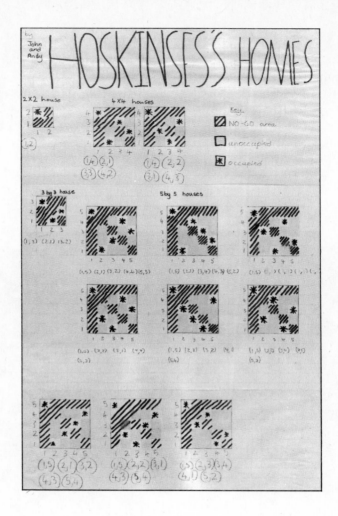

The results of the children's work were presented in a variety of ways: tables, scale drawings, plans, area 'maps', graphs, grids, lists and Venn diagrams. Below is a list of the maths involved in the project:

reading documents
area conservation
attributes
weight
scale
coordinates
direction
grids
problem solving
inventories
logic
number bases

ordering
sets
money
perspective
tables
rank order
investigations
matrices
maps
number work
plans

Follow-up

The follow-up activities were as varied as those in the initial project. The children drew plans of their own houses, and did further work on area conservation, different scales and enlargements. They investigated other number bases and looked at other uses of base 2. They also studied leaflets on overseas and inland postal rates.

Epilogue

Manuel went to see Pushkin. 'The others', he said 'they're throwing cushions at me. It's not safe inside the house.'
'It's not safe outside it, either,' said Pushkin. They went to tell Arthur about it.
'You must make a plan,' said Arthur 'and then you must write out some rules.'
'What are you going to do?' asked Pushkin.
'Sell tickets,' said Arthur.

Extract from *Arthur's Zoo*, written by Nicola Davies

59

Cylinders

The topic of cylinders was chosen because it was strictly mathematical. The children were introduced to the topic through a discussion on 'What is a cylinder?' They were then invited to make a collection of cylinders and from these the work developed. The maths involved included:

measuring	angles
constants/variables	
speed	volume
linear measurement	
area	shape
measuring diameter	
scale	'viewing'
circle properties	
ordering	structures
line properties	volume

VIVIENNE JAHANS

Children made a collection of cylinders, leading to work on measurement and classification.

The children were encouraged to order, partition, classify and generally consider the attributes of the cylinders.

The cylinders were ordered by height, diameter, rolling speed, thickness, and capacity.

The results were presented as Venn diagrams, Carroll diagrams, mappings and block graphs. Some examples of their work are presented here. Photocopiable sheets are given on pages 136 to 142.

Follow-up

Follow-up questions might include:
- Are there situations that can be represented by non-intersecting sets, using Venn diagrams, but not Carroll diagrams?
- How do you measure diameter?
- How did you define 'fast', and 'very fast'?

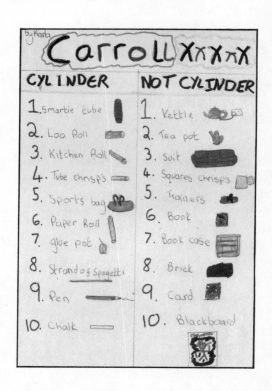

by Kasta

Carroll XⲀXⲀX

CYLINDER	NOT CYLINDER
1. Smartie tube	1. Kettle
2. Loo Roll	2. Tea pot
3. Kitchen Roll	3. Suit
4. Tube chrisps	4. Squares chrisps
5. Sports bag	5. Trainers
6. Paper Roll	6. Book
7. glue pot	7. Book case
8. Strand of Spagetti	8. Brick
9. Pen	9. Card
10. Chalk	10. Blackboard

The following activities are more suitable for older children:

● The children realised that the commercial tubes could be unrolled into parallelograms. This was developed into work involving perpendicular height and area.

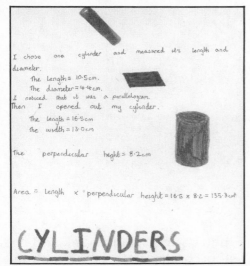

They also built cylinders from card and investigated constant-diameter/altered length.

● Volume was 'measured' by filling cylindrical objects with uniform solids. Of course, there was the problem of interstices but this was shelved for a later time. The children could have measured volume in a conventional way, in terms of cubic centimetres of liquid, but this would have imposed liquid measurement on to a class seeing volume in terms of discontinuous solids. They presented their results in graph form:

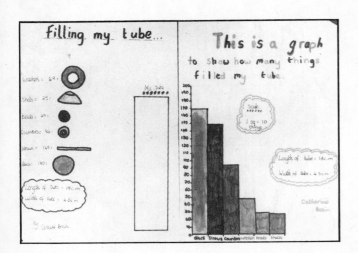

All the children were asked to evaluate their work. Not all of them, however, were at the stage where they could detach themselves sufficiently to do this.

Anglegrams

This activity was introduced by asking the children to put 5cm of water into a cylindrical coffee jar and tilt it at a 25° angle. They then measured the water level on each side of the cylinder.

Through their investigations they realised the relationship between the two measurements. One child said: 'Most of the measurements added up to 10 cm, except when the water went round the bottom it didn't.' When queried why, he responded: 'I don't know. It's almost like a negative amount. The higher side was more than 10 cm and the lower side was below the measuring-line, so it's like a minus quantity.'

The anglegrams were the children's own solution for linking angle to height, as shown below:

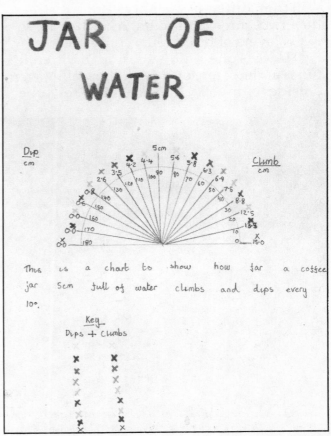

61

They also devised tilt diagrams:

Tube-viewing

This work was suggested by Marion Walters at the Association of Teachers of Mathematics Easter Conference, 1987.

The children measured the diameter of a tube and then looked at the bricks on the wall from different distances – one metre, then two, three, and so on, recording how many layers of bricks they could see.

Here is one child's account of different tubes at the same level from the wall: 'I went outside with Vicky. I took a toilet-roll tube, pencil, metre stick, rough book and chalk. First, I stood one metre away from the wall and counted the layers of bricks I could see through my tube. I kept going back a metre until I could see all of the layers of bricks. Vicky wrote up the results for me. It was quite exciting thinking about how many more layers you were going to see, and then finding if you were right.'

The results were presented as scattergrams and involved the use of scale and coordinates.

VIVIENNE JAHANS

After measuring the tube's diameter, the children counted the layers of bricks they could see.

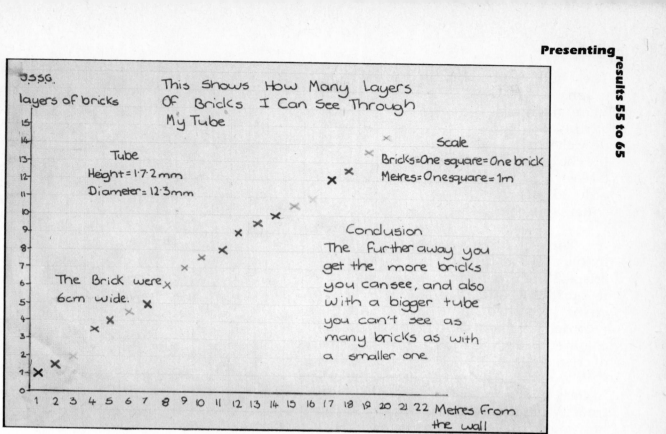

J.S.S.G.

layers of bricks

This Shows How Many Layers Of Bricks I Can See Through My Tube

Tube
Height = 1·7·2 mm
Diameter = 12·3mm

Scale
Bricks=One square= One brick
Metres= One square= 1m

The Brick were 6cm wide.

Conclusion
The further away you get the more bricks you can see, and also with a bigger tube you can't see as many bricks as with a smaller one.

Metres From the wall

A real-life situation

Crisps were chosen as a topic of investigation to emphasise the fact that maths can be derived from any part of the children's lives.

The children were invited to collect crisps packets, both empty and full, for investigation. Among the questions raised were: Which was the most popular flavour? How many packets were bought each week? Could we really differentiate between flavours? How much would a tonne of crisps cost, and would it be the same for all makes?

This topic differed from the others in that the teacher input was minimal and parents were involved. As well as providing the range of crisps, and information about prices, parents offered active support in the classroom, helping the children to make crisps. This involved costing raw materials (the potatoes), preparing them for cooking, frying the crisps and weighing them afterwards. The maths involved included:

weighing
fractions
ratio

measuring
proportions
grids

money
investigations
temperature
costing
counting
relationships

averages
angles
fixing variables
keys
percentage

VIVIENNE JAHANS

Results from the crisps topic are attractively displayed, showing the children's discoveries at a glance.

The results can be presented as follows:
graphs
Venn diagrams
attributes
flow charts
pie charts
tables
ordered lists
square 'pie charts'

Three children's accounts are as follows: 'We all brought in a packet of crisps. When we had found out 30 people's favourites, we did a pie chart. For weighing crisps, I weighed all the packets and recorded my results as a graph. We also coloured in a small square if we had a packet of crisps for lunch.'

'Every day, we would ask all the people in class if they had eaten crisps that lunch-time. When the week was up we could see how many packets were eaten each day.'

'The Venn diagram was interesting because I found that there was a difference between the flavours that younger children and "almost-grown-up" children liked.'

Some of the crisps results were presented as pie charts.

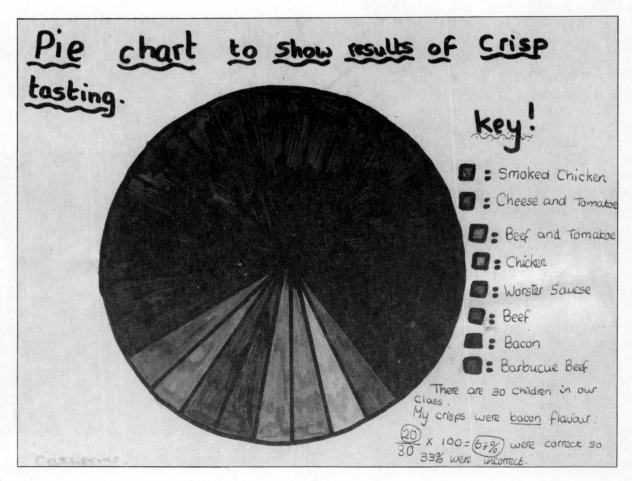

Pie chart to show results of crisp tasting.

key!
■ : Smoked Chicken
■ : Cheese and Tomatoe
■ : Beef and Tomatoe
■ : Chicken
■ : Worster Sauce
■ : Beef
■ : Bacon
■ : Barbucue Beef

There are 30 children in our class.
My crisps were bacon flavour.
$\frac{20}{30}$ × 100 = 67% were correct so 33% were incorrect.

64

Evaluation

The teacher must ensure that the children can understand the final form of their own and others' work, and they should be encouraged to discuss its effectiveness.

Information is more easily gleaned from displayed results, even if vicarious. The displays are there for reference, not as wall-coverings.

Block graphs, pie charts and square charts are quantitative: they display measurable quantities. Block graphs can be used for rank order. Carroll diagrams are non-quantitative, because they partition. Venn diagrams are also non-quantitative; they show relationships, interrelationships and absence of relationships. Graphs show patterns and mathematical relationships with some accuracy; they can be used for prediction. Scatter graphs show relationships, but cannot be used for predictions that require accuracy. Coordinates 'fix' a position accurately. Scale drawings are accurate representations; shape is preserved, as is direction, area and length; the actual measurements cannot be known unless the scale is known.

Prediction

The displays can be used for questions like these:

- What angle would produce a 9 cm tilt?
- How many children might eat crisps next Monday?
- What size cylinder would hold 22 beads?
- How many different six-by-six Hoskin grids do you think there are?

Conclusions

Our aim was to show how different approaches and topics colour the way results are presented. The work on crisps was essentially numerical, but it did not lend itself naturally to ordering, as the cylinder work did. The nub of the crisps work was statistical; that of the cylinder work was pattern (incorporating relationships and predictions); that of the Hoskin work was representation (scale, problem-solving, attributes, keys). The line-of-average could only be used in the crisps block graphs; the scattergrams were a necessity for the cylinder work; the Hoskin grids were the only way to deal with the problem of housing Hoskins.

Only by working on a variety of topics do children develop the skills of sifting through a range of techniques until they light upon those best suited to the work in hand.

The cylinder work involved ordering and pattern.

VIVIENNE JAHANS

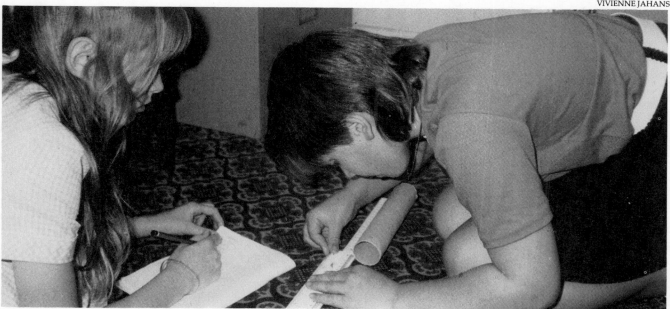

The new technology

The new technology

INTRODUCTION

CHRIS SUNLEY

The last ten years has seen a technological revolution which has affected all our lives. Most children now have a digital watch, most homes have a calculator and many also have a computer. In the world of work calculators and computers are widely accepted and used where speed, accuracy and efficiency are important.

The calculator revolution

The primary classroom has not escaped the influence of the micro-chip. Since schools first began to explore the use of the calculator in 1976, there has been a growing awareness and interest in the role of the calculator in the maths curriculum. The Shell project in the early 1980s did much to point the direction for the future, and their findings have been echoed by Cockcroft, the

HMI reports, and most recently by the School Curriculum Development Council in *Maths Today and Tomorrow*.

For many teachers, the calculator is limited to checking answers which have been reached using the traditional method, or is seen as a device that will erode children's knowledge of tables, number bonds and mental skills. Sometimes it is seen as yet another aspect of mathematics to be added to an already overcrowded syllabus. Such understandable fears clearly show not only the apprehension of teachers, but also a general lack of understanding about the potential of the calculator.

Recent studies have all indicated that using a calculator does not stop children learning tables; for many it provides the necessary challenge, reinforcement and encouragement to learn them. Nor does the calculator make the learning of number bonds and tables redundant. It is still much quicker to recall that six sevens are forty-two than to find a calculator and key in the problem.

Just using a calculator does not tell children what sums to do, which buttons to press, or whether the final answer is likely to be right. These decisions must still be made by the child and the corresponding skills still need to be taught.

However, we must recognise that the calculator can perform some functions more quickly and efficiently, and we cannot ignore its widespread use in the world of work, where a correct answer is far more important than an inaccurate but neatly laid-out long division sum.

Adults are far more likely to use a calculator or their own personal method which they understand and which gives the correct answer. Because these methods do not fit the traditional pattern of maths teaching, they are often called non-standard recording methods.

Many children already use such methods. Most teachers have met children who tackle 12 × 17 as a repeated addition sum and get the right answer. They use a method they feel comfortable with even though they may have been taught long multiplication.

Some aspects of primary mathematics will assume a greater importance once the calculator is used freely in the classroom and teachers will need to be aware of this.

The most important of these must be

Decimal fractions must be explained early on.

mental calculations. The ready availability of a calculator does not mean it must be used for every calculation; just when the numbers are too large or difficult for the child to handle mentally.

The skills of approximation and estimation are dependent on a firm understanding of place value. Finding out which two consecutive numbers make 2070 when multiplied together, uses an initial estimate and the power of the calculator to arrive at an increasingly accurate answer. Without a calculator this kind of work would be beyond the scope of most primary children.

Decimal fractions are likely to occur earlier, as calculators do not give whole number remainders. Teachers will need to deal with questions about the decimal fraction, the number of digits in the display and the relevance of the answer to the question, particularly in real life problems.

Directed numbers will also appear, often unexpectedly, when children subtract with a constant function or press the $\boxed{-}$ key instead of the $\boxed{=}$ key. The calculator can be used to introduce this new area which, when related to the extended number line, is within the reach of older primary school children.

The computer

Whilst the calculator revolution has been slowly but steadily growing, the sudden impetus of the computer left many teachers baffled and even hostile to this new, costly and sometimes temperamental technology. Early software tended to push the computer into a corner of the classroom where children took turns to check tables and number bonds. Some reinforcement software may be useful, but limiting the computer's use in this way ignores its real potential within the primary curriculum.

The interactive nature of good software makes it an ideal way of presenting and introducing investigations and problem-solving activities, where children work away from the computer, returning only to test and evaluate their findings.

The use of LOGO (a programming language designed for educational use), either in its simplest form as Turtle graphics, or as the full programming language, offers children a problem-solving environment where they are in control of their own work.

The computer's ability to handle large amounts of data and to present it in different ways provides an excellent vehicle for children to collect real data and then collate, tabulate and represent it in a mathematical context.

If the computer is generally used to support the work already going on in the classroom, it may appear less of a threat to the curriculum than the calculator. However, both pose many new questions and open up new horizons for the primary curriculum. This chapter will look at some of the most important issues and suggest ways in which this new technology can both enrich and stimulate work in the primary mathematics curriculum.

Get to know your calculator

As with all equipment, a good working understanding of the calculator is vital if you are to get the maximum benefit from using it in the classroom. This section looks at some of the important features of the calculator.

Types of calculator

The name 'four-function calculator' describes the simple calculators which can be identified by the small number of keys and the price, which is usually less than £5. Scientific calculators have 20 or more keys labelled tan, log, and so on. These are generally used from secondary school

onwards, but can be used in the primary classroom.

Although calculators are all designed for the same basic tasks, they do not all work in the same way. With a mixture of scientific and basic calculators it is possible to get different answers for the same calculation, both of which are correct!

This difference can be demonstrated by keying in:

$$4 \boxed{+} 2 \boxed{\times} 5 \boxed{=}$$

The scientific calculator uses algebraic logic to give the answer 14. It rewrites the

First children must understand how to use the functions.

problem, taking the multiplication part first:

$$4 + (2 \times 5) = 14$$

The four-function calculator uses arithmetic logic and works out the problem in the order it is entered.

$$4 + 2 \times 5 = 30$$

A calculator using algebraic logic can be made to operate as an arithmetic calculator by pressing the 'equals' key between each calculation. Our example would be keyed in as:

4 $\boxed{+}$ 2 $\boxed{=}$ $\boxed{\times}$ 5 $\boxed{=}$ 30

With older children such differences can be used to introduce order of priorities for calculations.

The constant function

An interesting and very useful feature found on most calculators is the constant function, which allows the same operation to be repeated using a single key press. This is useful for building up tables, working with number lines, counting backwards and forwards in ones, fives (and so on), finding squares, dividing by repeated subtraction, multiplying by repeated addition and investigational work.

There are two major ways to create a constant. The first is the direct approach where the constant is created by repeatedly pressing the 'equals' key. For example, to make an 'add 2' constant starting from the 6 key:

6 $\boxed{+}$ 2 $\boxed{=}$$\boxed{=}$$\boxed{=}$ 8, 10, 12

The second system works the other way round. The constant is entered first and the starting number added later:

2 $\boxed{+}$$\boxed{+}$ 6 $\boxed{=}$$\boxed{=}$$\boxed{=}$ 8, 10, 12

Here the constant is created by pressing the 'add' key twice in succession.

Although the first approach is simpler to follow and more easily understood by children, they may use it inadvertently by pressing the equals key twice accidentally.

Clearing information

All calculators have some method of clearing all information as well as clearing only the number entered last (clear entry). Some calculators have two separate keys: $\boxed{AC}$ clears the entire calculator memory and display, whilst $\boxed{CE}$ clears only the last entry and leaves the displayed total and memory intact. Other types have the two functions combined on a single key, $\boxed{C/CE}$. One press clears the last entry and two presses clears the entire calculator.

Keys and displays

The layout of the calculator keyboard is a matter of choice but there should be a clear pattern which separates the number keys from the operator keys ($+ \div \times -$) and other function and memory keys.

Key size is important, however, and credit card calculators are too small for primary school children. Look for large keys which are well spaced and clearly marked.

There are also different types of key materials. The best keys are made from rigid plastic with a soft, positive touch. Keys which click when pressed can give trouble after prolonged use and are easily mis-pressed. Some cheaper calculators have keys made of a rubber type material. Whilst having a soft touch, they have a less positive feel than plastic keys, and they can be damaged by sharp instruments like scissors and compasses.

Select calculators which have the grey, liquid-crystal display. Not only do they consume much less power, but they are also easier to see in all lighting conditions. Aim for the largest possible display, particularly for young children.

When buying calculators for school use, consider the following features in approximate order of priority:

- key size and composition,
- display size and information given,
- constant function operation,
- clear key operation,
- other keys ($\sqrt{}$ +/− 1/× %)
- three-, four-key memory,
- solar or battery-powered against cost,
- protective case.

You will find that different models from the same manufacturer use the same conventions for constant functions, clear entry, and so on. Therefore it is a good idea to stick to the same manufacturer, if not the same model, within a single age range or school.

Starting with the calculator

Digital displays

Although young children are used to seeing digital displays and pressing buttons on televisions, video-recorders, digital watches and computers, familiarity does not necessarily bring understanding.

To introduce young children to the calculator, ask them to key in simple numbers like their door or telephone number. This helps them to relate the digital numbers on the display to the written arabic numerals.

The teacher can then key in a number, and ask the children to press the key or keys which put the same number into the display. Some children will have difficulty with the numbers two and five, which can look very similar in digital form.

Children build patterns with blocks which reflect the numbers appearing on their calculator displays.

This activity can be extended by relating the pattern on the calculator display to more concrete materials, such as beads or Multilink apparatus.

eg calculator display 323234

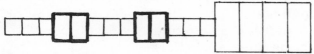

Pattern in blocks

Introducing the constant function

The constant function should be introduced early in the primary school. The teacher may need to set the constant to start with, but the children will soon learn the skill. Begin with a 'plus one' constant, and encourage the children to predict the next number on the display either orally or on a number line.

With older children the same facility can be used to count backwards or forwards in twos, threes, tens and so on. It is also particularly useful when counting across tens, hundreds or thousands, as the children can see the digits changing.

The same feature can be programmed into a computer, giving children even greater control over the counting and speed of display.

There are many games involving the use of the constant function which can be played at several levels. For example, children can practise addition by the teacher setting up a secret constant.

The child has a piece of paper marked:

IN   OUT

Any number is pressed, say 5, and recorded in the 'IN' column. Pressing $=$ gives a number which is written in the

73

Calculator games and activities are an enjoyable way of developing mathematical understanding.

'OUT' column. Without pressing the 'clear' key, a new number is entered and the process repeated until the child has discovered what the constant is.

eg secret constant 2

IN	OUT
5	7
8	10

Once the children have learned to set their own constants, they can work in pairs with one child setting a problem for the other to solve. For older and more able children the constant can be changed to include subtraction, multiplication by 10 or 0.5, and division by 2, 10 or even 43.

The keyboard

There is no need to explain the use of every key on the calculator. However, even some of the older children will ask where the 'share' button is, and work will be needed to familiarise them with the four-function buttons, the digit keys and the 'equals' and 'decimal point' keys.

It is also important to introduce the 'clear entry' and 'clear all' keys to older children, explaining how they can be used when an error is made to avoid re-keying the complete problem.

Mathematical language

An activity which can be used at all levels requires the children to work out the answers to a range of verbal problems which use a range of mathematical language:
● Seven add eight equals—
● Nine times six makes—
● Fourteen subtract four leaves—
● Find the total of eight, five and nine.
● What is twenty divided by five?
● What number is nineteen less than forty-six?
● Find the sum of three, eleven and fifteen.

It is important that children not only write the answer, but also which keys they have pressed. This gives the teacher a good idea of a child's understanding of the language of mathematics. The idea can be extended to include a whole range of other mathematical problems and language: for example, find the perimeter of an 18cm square.

Some calculator keys will form natural starting points for new work or investigations. For instance, many children will ask what the 'square root' key does. Ask them to key in some perfect squares (16, 49) and then press the 'square root' key. Can they spot what has happened?

Place value and the calculator

The calculator is an embodiment of the whole place value number system, and can be used in many activities to introduce, reinforce and check children's understanding of this important area of mathematics. However, it cannot replace traditional structural apparatus and practical work. The two can and must exist side by side in the primary classroom.

The use of the calculator alongside the number line has already been mentioned, but this type of activity can be extended to number lines involving whole numbers, tenths and even hundredths:

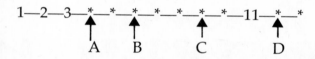

Count along the number line and add each number using the calculator:

A.....
B.....   Total.....
C.....
D.....   Check answer: 31

Reading numbers

When asked to write in figures a number given in words many children will make simple mistakes due to poor place value understanding, such as writing 10042 for 142.

'Reading numbers' is a simple and useful activity which reinforces and checks children's understanding of this important skill.

Write each of these numbers down and then add them up using a calculator:

one hundred and six
three hundred and twenty two
five hundred and sixteen
one thousand and sixty six

Check answer: 2010

The activity can be matched to the children's age and ability, extended with sets containing different kinds of numbers:

one kilogram and 340 grams
two and a half kilograms
one pound twenty seven
sixty seven pence
one and a half
two and three quarters
six and seven tenths
seven point three eight

A similar activity can be used to reinforce children's work in rounding numbers. Round the following numbers to the nearest ten and add them together using the calculator:

356   487   315   23   749

Check answer: 1940

'Reading numbers' emphasises place value.

In all these activities it is important that children write down the numbers they are adding together. This will enable the teacher to see where mistakes have been made and to pin-point any misunderstandings.

Forecast and check

This activity is particularly useful in place value work where it encourages children to look at the pattern of number by forecasting or estimating an answer, and then checking the answer with a calculator.

This activity can be used over a wide range of place value work. The examples below give some useful starting points. See page 143 for a photocopiable sheet.

Number	Operation	Forecast	Check
23	+20		
23	×10		
23	×20		
230	10		
23	10		
99	+ 1		
103	− 5		
999	+ 2		

The constant function can be useful in this activity. In the first of these examples, a 'plus 20' constant can be set so that when children are checking their forecasts they have only to key in the number and press the 'equals' key to get the answer.

Please may I have

Mathematical games are now an important part of most primary classrooms, and the calculator has opened up some new possibilities which can motivate and encourage children whilst helping to reinforce new skills and concepts.

'Please may I have' is played by two children who each have a calculator. Each player enters a personal secret starting number with a given number of digits. If there are three digits then each player tries to get his calculator to show a number equal to or larger than 1,000. If there are four digits, then each player tries to make a number greater than or equal to 10,000, and so on.

Once the numbers are entered into the calculators, the players take it in turns to call out a number between one and nine. The value of the number is given to the player asking for it and taken from the other player. If a player has, say, two threes, they must both be given as their value (for example 353 would give 303).

'Forecast and check' develops estimation skills whilst reinforcing understanding of place value.

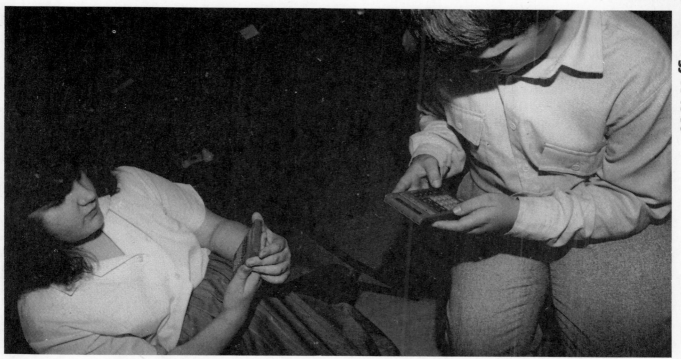

Playing calculator games like 'Please may I have' motivates children while developing mathematical skills.

If a player doesn't have any of the numbers asked for, the play changes sides. If neither player can reach 1,000 (or 10,000), the loser is the first player to be reduced to zero.

PLAYER 1		PLAYER 2
468	secret starting numbers	392

Please may I have your sixes

| 408 | You get 60 | 452 |

Please may I have your sevens

| 408 | You get nothing | 452 |

Please may I have your fours

| 8 | You get 400 | 852 |

Please may I have your eights

| 808 | You get 800 | 52 |

Please may I have your eights

| 0 | You get 808 | 860 |

The game can be extended for older children by asking them to make four-, five- or six-digit numbers, or even starting with decimal fractions and adding to make one. It is interesting to watch the strategies they use.

Place invaders

The main aim of this game is to reduce a given number to zero by subtracting numbers from the different place value columns one number at a time. The numbers subtracted should reduce a single column to zero each time.

Start numbering	Key presses	Display
364	⊟ 4 ⊜	360
	⊟ 60 ⊜	300
	⊟ 300 ⊜	0

A more difficult version asks children to add digits, one column at a time, to reach 1,000:

364	⊞ 6 ⊜	370
	⊞ 40 ⊜	410
	⊞ 90 ⊜	500
	⊞ 500 ⊜	1000

Again it is important that children keep a record of their play so that mistakes and misunderstandings can be spotted and rectified. A duplicated playing grid makes this simpler.

Like all good calculator games, 'Place invaders' can be used at many levels: it can be extended to include larger starting numbers, numbers containing decimal fractions and tackling digits in descending or ascending order.

To make the game more challenging, use a scoring system: children are given 100 points for each new number, and lose ten points for each try including mistakes. A complete mistake which makes the game unplayable returns the player to the last start number, but leaves the score as it was – an incentive for accurate keying!

Bullseye

For children looking at decimal fractions, 'Bullseye' introduces the idea that numbers to the right of the decimal point have a decreasing value. The game can be played by a single child, a group, or even the whole class. Each player needs a calculator and page 144.

A target number and a start number are given, and players must find which number to multiply the start number by to give the

In 'Place invaders' a number must be reduced to zero.

target number as closely as possible: eg target 100; starting number 23

Start number	Estimate	Calculator answer
23	6	138
	4	92
	5	115
	4.5	103.5
	4.4	101.2
	4.3	98.9
	4.35	100.05

Children must record their work as they go, as it soon becomes impossible to remember which numbers have been tried and the answers that were obtained. To simplify keying, use the constant function to multiply automatically the trial number by the start number.

'Bullseye' also introduces the concept of accuracy. Different levels of play can introduce greater accuracy. For the example above:

Level 1	between 90 and 110
Level 2	between 99 and 101
Level 3	between 99.5 and 100.5
Level 4	between 99.9 and 100.1
Level 5	between 99.99 and 100.01

More calculator games

Beat the calculator

It is important, from the outset, to show children that the calculator is often far slower than the human brain once a concept has been understood or number bonds learned to the point of instant recall.

An ideal activity to emphasise this, and to encourage children to learn tables and basic number bonds, is 'Beat the calculator'.

The teacher prepares a pack of cards, tailored to the age and ability of the children concerned, which could show number bond facts, tables, simple additions or a sequence of operations.
For example:
$3 \times 7 =$
$26 + 30 =$
$48 \div 6 =$
eight plus one half of sixteen
the cost of three loaves at 43p each
$1256 + 4000$.

Children play in pairs with one calculator. One child *must* use the calculator for every problem, while the other *must not* use it at all. Cards are turned over one at a time and the first child to get the right answer wins the card. When the questions are finished, the child with the most cards wins.

Children soon realise that the calculator is not always quicker, especially if they do not know how to use it properly.

Touchdown

'Touchdown' can be used with young children to practise number bond skills up to ten or twenty. It can also be extended to reinforce all of the four number operations, using larger numbers or those with decimal fractions.

Two players share one calculator, photocopy page 145 and a set of cards with numbers written on them. The first player turns over the top card, keys the number into the calculator, then returns the card to the bottom of the pack.

The other player turns over the top card and tries to make the calculator display show this new number in one operation. If she is successful, she keeps the card; otherwise it is returned to the bottom of the pack. The calculator and play then passes to

Children must realise that it is not always quicker to use the calculator.

'Touchdown' can be played at various levels to reinforce number bond skills, using whole numbers or decimals.

the first player. The calculator display is not cleared between turns, so the last display is the starting point for the next player. The winner is the one with the most cards.

In order to encourage the use of multiplication, division, and even square roots, an extra turn can be given to a player using any of these operations. Extra cards showing the numbers 1 and 0 are also useful for emphasising particular skills and concepts.

Target

'Target' encourages children to plan strategies whilst reinforcing number bond skills. It can be used with groups or individuals.

Children are asked to get various numbers into the calculator display using only certain digits and operators: eg make the number 2 appear in the calculator display using only these keys:

$\boxed{4}\ \boxed{3}\ \boxed{\times}\ \boxed{-}\ \boxed{=}$

$2 \rightarrow \square\square\square\square\square\square\square\square\square$

The number of key presses is limited by the boxes on the playing grid, although the

players do not have to use all the boxes. Each key may be pressed as often as necessary.

Children should be encouraged to try many different approaches and the strategies they adopt can provide useful insights into their thinking and method of working.

The players should try out their ideas on the calculator as sometimes they do not give the expected answer, particularly where there is an order of priority for operations.

In 'Target' number bond skills are developed further.

Four in a row

The use of the calculator requires a new emphasis on the skills of estimation and approximation. Before using the calculator for a problem, children should have an idea of the size of answer they need. This does not mean every calculation should be worked out in rough first, but children should be able to see whether the calculator answer is likely to be correct.

'Four in a row' is a game which encourages children to make estimates. Two children, with one calculator and two sets of coloured counters, are given a set of numbers which they must use to make the numbers in the playing grid (see page 146). If they correctly select the two numbers which make their target number, they cover that square with their own coloured counter.

The aim is to make a line of four counters of the same colour in any direction. At the easiest level this game tests number bond skills with the calculator being used either to allow children to try out numbers or to check answers. Some 'rogue' numbers which cannot be made from the numbers supplied helps to make the game more interesting!

To make the game more difficult, include different mathematical concepts and skills, such as different levels of addition and subtraction, different levels of division and multiplication, equivalent fractions, numbers with decimal fractions, or multiplying and dividing by ten, a hundred, and so on.

'Four in a row' is another game which exercises number bond skills whilst encouraging the skill of estimation.

Investigations and problem solving

Although investigational work and problem solving have been part of the primary maths curriculum for a long time, they have often been restricted due to the computational problems or the numbers used. However, thanks to the calculator, this work has become accessible to many more children.

Investigations

Faced with an investigation the first approach is usually to have a go and try something. The computational power of the calculator allows many examples to be tried when looking for a pattern, and helps children's attention to remain focused on the problem rather than the arithmetic involved. Confidence is increased, too, by the knowledge that the calculator gives correct answers.

Although the calculator itself cannot help a child to identify a pattern, this increased confidence and ease of computation makes the task less onerous. The calculator also enables a pattern to be extended and tested without too much effort being expended on routine calculations.

Once identified, a pattern must be tested: does it work with large or small

numbers? Again, the power of the calculator enables very large, small or awkward numbers to be tried with ease and confidence.

The pattern should then be explained to others. At the primary stage there is no need for algebraic solutions but children must be encouraged to explain and share their results. The resulting discussions, often using the calculator to show what has been done, will lead children to a greater understanding.

The following activities show the power of the calculator in this type of work, and also help with estimation skills. Children must record their own work.

Multiples of 11
Work out the following multiples of 11 using a calculator:

13×11
27×11
45×11
73×11
98×11

Look at the answers and try to find a link between the start number and the answer. Can you find a way of calculating multiples of 11 without actually multiplying any numbers? Does it work for larger numbers?

Interesting patterns are also created by dividing numbers by 11.

Box numbers

Use the digits 1, 2, 3, 4 once only to make the following target numbers:

☐ ☐ ☐+ ☐ ☐

The answer is 37.

☐ ☒ ☐ ☐ ☐

Make the largest possible answer.

Try to get as close as possible to the target number:

☐ ☐ ☒ ☐ ☐

Target 500.

Problem solving

Children often find it difficult to relate the problems done in school to those found in the real world. This may be because the problems are not relevant to the children's experiences, or the numbers have been carefully selected to give easy calculations. In real life cue words like 'share' and 'how many' may be missing, and the numbers found in real situations are often more difficult to handle or do not give easy answers.

The calculator is no magical panacea to problem solving work. Children must still be able to decide what sums to do and be able to interpret their answers. But the calculator will give children the confidence to have a go, the ability to handle realistic data, and the knowledge that the calculator will provide correct answers.

In solving real problems the calculator gives children the confidence to try out solutions.

Many starting points can come from the children's own questions and experience:

How many names are there in the telephone directory? How many tiles or blocks are there in the hall floor? How many seconds are there in a day? How many seconds have you lived for? How old were you, or will you be, when you have lived for a million hours?

The following problem, which can easily arise in shopping surveys and topic work, requires careful selection of units and interpretation of the answer:

Which packet of soap powder is the best buy?
Economy size: 2.2 kg at £2.73
Standard size: 920 gm at 93p

Without a calculator this would be a difficult problem for most primary children, but once the problem has been turned into a sum it can be solved easily using the calculator. Like all good problem solving work, it will also give rise to much discussion.

The digital watch

The majority of children now own a watch and many of these are digital. At home children are surrounded by digital readouts from alarm clocks, video-recorders and timing devices.

The analogue watch or clock stresses the cyclical nature of time, with each hour and day following the same pattern. With a digital watch it is possible that children no longer regard the hours as cyclical, and teachers need to be aware of this.

A digital 'day-line' may help, provided that it is circular with the end joining the beginning. For younger children this could be displayed with the half and quarter hours marked, and minutes could be added for older pupils.

People who wear digital watches lay great stress upon the accuracy of the time. Instead of nearly half past ten, the time will be given as 10.28. It could be argued that the digital watch will undermine the idea of rounding off times to the nearest five minutes, and the whole concept of half or three-quarters of an hour could be in

The analogue clock-face is useful as an introduction to fractions, right angles and turning.

danger. This may affect other work in maths.

The analogue clock-face is used by teachers for many mathematical activities. The quarter hours provide an introduction to simple fractions and right angles.

Investigations into turning, and even vocabulary such as 'clockwise' and 'anti-clockwise', may all involve the analogue clock-face.

There is no way that teachers can hold back the use of digital watches and their growing presence in our lives must affect not only what we teach children in the primary school but also the way in which it is taught.

Using the computer

Access to the school's computer may be limited by a timetable or the curriculum as a whole and so it is important that teachers make the best possible use of this computer time.

As educational software has developed to encompass the whole curriculum, the idea that computers were only for mathematicians has, fortunately, become less prominent. However there is still much software which can be used within the maths curriculum.

Computers and Cockcroft

It is possible to look at mathematics software from a number of different viewpoints, and the MEP maths pack produced in 1984 makes some helpful comparisons between the teaching styles outlined in Cockcroft and uses of mathematical software.

Some software can aid the teacher in the traditional role of explaining or reinforcing a new concept. A program like *Data Show* (NORICC), for example, which draws simple graphs and pie charts, can be used over a wide age range and usefully incorporated into maths work at many levels.

A program called *Halving* shows a variety of ways to halve a square. Although the program is non-interactive it can be stopped at any point and used as a basis for group or class discussion. It can also be used as stimulus for practical work and to encourage pupils to look at the concept of a half in many ways.

Halving could also be placed in the next category of discussion. Like many calculator activities the computer can be an ideal stimulus in getting children to talk about their work. Many of these interactive programs should be used as a group activity which will encourage children to discuss their response.

Concept reinforcement

Like many calculator activities, the computer can be an ideal stimulus for encouraging children to talk about their work. Many of the interactive programs should be used as a group activity.

Predict (SMILE) asks for a series of numbers, devises a rule which links them in a particular way, and then asks children to spot the rule. This creates a learning situation where children discuss their predictions and results, make new suggestions, and then try them out. All of these activities require a wide range of number skills.

There is a plethora of software designed for children to practise various skills. Much of it is designed to reinfore basic number bonds and tables practice. For example, *Trains* (Anita Straker) can provide useful motivation for children to practise basic number skills.

The computer's graphical powers are valuable within this type of software, where playing grids, shapes, fractions and clock-faces, quickly and accurately reproduced, can provide examples matched to the children's ability.

However, it is worth looking further than these basic reinforcement programs to packages which help to reinforce specific concepts. Many of these programs exercise mental skills in a game situation, where the computer encourages children to work out answers in their heads, rather than using paper and pencil calculations.

Blocks (NORICC) is similar to the calculator 'Four in a row' game, giving the children a playing grid and simulating the throwing of three dice. The numbers displayed must be combined in some way to make one of the numbers on the grid.

Apart from reinforcing simple number bonds, older and more able children can use different operators, brackets and even powers to produce particular numbers.

Investigations and problem solving

However, it is within investigations and problem solving that the computer can add a new dimension to the primary maths curriculum.

A program like *Teashop* (NORICC) enables younger children to use simple mathematical skills in a situation not easily duplicated in the classroom. In simulating a real-life situation, children can experiment and make errors without the risk that real encounters would produce.

As children grow older a wider range of software becomes available which enables them to experience problem solving activities in situations which they cannot experience in real life. Although this software is not specifically mathematical it can be used within an integrated topic.

Adventure Island (Ginn) places children on a deserted island from which they must escape. This requires group decisions about distances to be travelled, maps to be coordinated, food to be carried and time to rest, as well as solving particular problems on the way. As in real life, wrong decisions can lead to disastrous results, but the computer allows children to try different strategies in safety.

Other packages, like *Spacex* (4Mation), *Mary Rose* (Ginn), *Cars – Maths in Motion* (Cambridge Software House) and *Saqqara* (Ginn), have a different emphasis but all place children in problem-solving situations.

Finally, the computer provides an excellent interactive medium for investigational work. For example, *Pattern* (NORICC) starts with simple questions about triangular numbers where children can work away from the computer, build a pattern and finally test their findings at the computer.

Spirals (SMILE) investigates open and closed spirals and again makes use of the computer's graphics. It involves children in formulating and testing hypotheses about

The screen turtle, like the floor turtle, develops an awareness of length, angle and space.

the shapes that will be produced from a number of different variables.

Only one of the teaching styles listed by Cockcroft has no direct computer parallel. Appropriate practical work should never be replaced with time at the computer. Structural apparatus, real objects, paper, pencils, scissors, sticky paper and compasses still have a vital part in developing children's mathematical skills and understanding.

Content-free software

All the software mentioned so far is designed and written for a specific purpose. Although different options may be available, the learning environment is strictly controlled by the parameters of the program. This is not the case with content-free software.

Turtle graphics

Content-free software offers the user an almost unlimited number of activities, many of which contain a strong mathematical content. Probably the most widely known is LOGO.

LOGO is a programming language specifically designed for educational use. In primary schools today it exists in two forms: turtle graphics, which is part of the full LOGO programming language, is the commonest form. *Dart* (AUCBE) and *LOGO Challenge* (Longmans) are examples of this type of software.

Turtle graphics enable children to develop simple commands to move a floor turtle in any direction. The floor turtle is a wheeled vehicle directly controlled by computer instructions sent through a linking cable or infra-red beam. It can also draw a line to leave a record of its path. Even young children soon devise their own procedures to make the turtle move in a particular direction and draw different shapes.

These activities help children to develop an awareness of space, length, angle and turn. For example, working out the commands to draw a square develops a basic understanding of the properties of the square.

As the children's ability to steer the floor turtle develops, they will make a natural transition to the screen where the same commands guide a screen turtle.

Children will soon begin to look for methods to speed up their drawing and store commands. As these needs arise the children can be introduced to REPEAT loops, procedures and simple variables. The procedures can be saved on to tape or disk and reloaded when the child uses the computer again.

This development cannot be forced at any stage, but must be taken at the child's speed. As skills develop, children do not need to work on the computer all the time. They can work away from the computer, planning and drawing on squared paper and writing their own procedures.

There are no right or wrong solutions. If the required shape is drawn, the method is correct, even though the teacher may be able to suggest improvements.

It is worth considering a full LOGO implementation, such as LOGOTRON, which incorporates turtle graphics whilst adding many other text and arithmetical commands. Children can build their own procedures to find the average of a set of numbers, write text on the screen, use colour and make music.

Databases

A database is another form of content-free software. For young children a program such as *Factfile* (Cambridge Micro Software) provides a simple introduction to creating, editing and searching data. Used with *Picfile* it can be used to draw simple graphs and display information in a number of ways.

As children's skills improve they will require a larger and more sophisticated database like *Grass* (Newman) or *Find* (RESOURCE). These allow more data to be stored, more complex searches and sorts, and they provide a wider range of statistical options.

Databases allow data to be stored, edited, sorted and searched, and can be used across the curriculum.

Histograms, bar graphs and pie charts can be drawn easily on the screen and reproduced on a printer, encouraging children to look at their data in a number of different ways, trying different types of graphs and data groupings.

This type of software is not primarily mathematical, and can be used across the whole curriculum. However, most databases will contain some numerical data which children will want to compare, contrast and explore.

It may not be possible, either economically or logistically, to explore and develop all the areas described above at the same time. Teachers will need to evaluate software with care to see if it will enhance work already covered or provide children with new experiences and challenges not available from traditional resources.

Children can print out results recorded on screen.

Organising the new technology

There is no need to purchase hundreds of calculators for use throughout a school. Each class should have five or six calculators, with a central school resource pool to make the class number up to a full or half class set. In larger schools, you may need more than one central pool.

Calculator lessons should not appear on the timetable, or be reserved for the end of term or a special 'treat'. Although there may be some class or group work involved when introducing calculators or specific functions, children should be able to use one whenever their work requires it.

89

Therefore access is important and calculators should not be locked away in cupboards or drawers. They are actually cheaper than many of the books displayed for all to use and read!

The computer poses greater problems, especially when there may be only one or two to serve the needs of an entire school.

Where short programs are being used for specific concepts or reinforcement it may be a good idea for classes to have access through a timetable. This should allow use for at least half a day at a time, as an hour here or there is of very limited value.

When a class begins to explore the use of LOGO, databases, word-processing or simulation programs, they will need the computer for half a term or longer. Children will gain more from a concentrated use over a shorter period than odd sessions throughout the year.

Software needs careful organisation. Master copies should never be available for general use unless absolutely necessary and documentation should always accompany the software.

Children benefit more from using the computer a lot over a short period, rather than intermittently.

Evaluating children's progress

Evaluating children's progress

INTRODUCTION

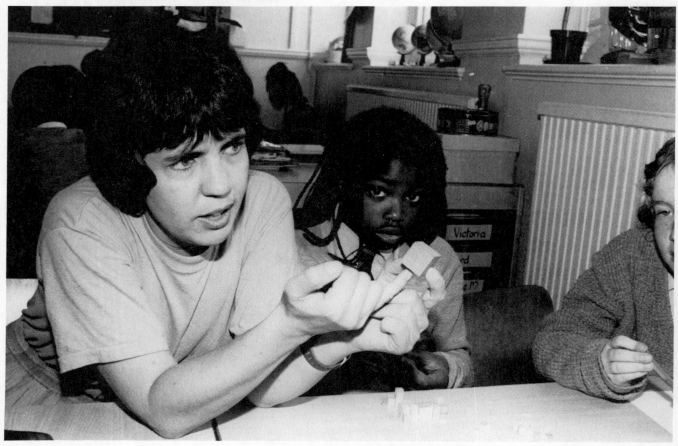

Assessment is an essential element of the teaching process and without it progress could not be ensured. It is often an informal process which is carried out 'automatically', but increasingly there are pressures to formalise the process.

Where schools are dependent on a published scheme for the maths curriculum, the need for formal assessment and recording procedures is not so obvious. We know which point each child has reached in the scheme, and whether sections have been missed or different activities introduced to reinforce specific ideas. Many schemes currently on the market have introduced their own record-keeping systems which provide a record of the work tackled through the scheme, although these are usually in the style of a checklist and the amount of detail gained from them can be very limited.

However, the quality of the informal assessment may be very high, and could be lost during the process of formalising assessment and recording techniques. In particular, any system of recording progress needs to be simple to use and to interpret, yet this very simplicity can lower the quality of the information. Our knowledge of the child will remain as good, but the information transferred to a record may be trite by comparison. This is an important consideration when devising a recording scheme within a school.

There must be a balance between the need for informative records which reflect the quality of the teacher's knowledge of the child, and the need for clear records which do not make unreasonable demands in terms of time for recording information and for reading it.

For assessment and recording to be effective the school must decide its priorities. *What* does it want to assess? *Why* does it want to assess? *How* does it want to assess?

It is vital that the type of evaluation of children's progress ties in with the type of work undertaken. Most evaluation techniques are specific to the child and the situation; if a child gets a good mark on a spelling test you cannot assume that he will be good at punctuation. Essentially the results of any test only tell you how a child coped with the questions in that test on that day.

Until comparatively recently, assessment in mathematics meant written tests. However, work over the past few years has introduced new techniques and considerably broadened the concept of assessment. In particular, the work of the Assessment of Performance Unit (APU) and the Concepts in Secondary Mathematics and Science project have built up knowledge and awareness of a variety of techniques, which can be applied to a wider concept of mathematics teaching and learning.

Research still continues in this area, much of it involving individual testing, where a teacher works in depth with one child. In particular, methods are being devised for assessing investigational work which is taking an important place in the mathematics curriculum.

There are many different aspects of mathematical understanding, and they need to be evaluated in different ways; some, such as those addressed by the traditional maths tests, are easier to assess than others. These have been designed to assess understanding of specific skills and concepts.

Maths assessment once involved only written tests, but assessment techniques have broadened.

In planning a curriculum, the role of assessment is to follow the route of the mathematics and not to lead it. If we are aware that certain items are to be tested at the end of a section of work, then it is tempting to teach to those specific goals. This leads to a restricted curriculum.

An added dimension of assessment is that you can ascertain the effectiveness of both your own teaching and the learning process. It is only too easy, without formal assessment procedures, to assume that everything you have taught has been learned and understood by your pupils.

If formal assessment is to take an increasingly important place in the curriculum, then the facilities must be made available for teachers to develop these techniques in a realistic setting. This has wider implications for staffing in primary schools. It is not realistic to ask teachers to undertake this type of work within the normal classroom situation, without appropriate support in terms of staffing and time available.

In the following section the possibility of assessing practical activities in the style adopted by the APU is discussed. This centrally funded team have attempted to make their methods available, but it must be remembered that they were able to work in a one-to-one situation with children, often for as much as 40 minutes at a time. Clearly such methods would be quite impractical in the normal school setting. So much time would be spent assessing children that there would be no time left for teaching.

Assessment is not an easy aspect of teaching, and incorporating a formal assessment plan into a school curriculum takes time. The following ideas and strategies have proved useful and are the most easily absorbed into classroom practice.

Practical testing

Objectives

To evaluate the pupil's understanding through practical work.

Our aim is to provide an opportunity for children to do some mathematics and discuss their experience of the process. It should provide an experience in which they can show what they can do rather than what they can write down.

Level of development

This method can be applied throughout the age range. The tasks chosen must be appropriate to each child, so that they are not placed in a situation in which they feel they cannot reasonably attempt the task.

Classroom organisation

The idea of practical testing is not new. There have been various curriculum projects which have incorporated it in the form of check-ups on a child's progress. Some are based on the experiments Piaget used in his clinical work, which have been adapted for the school situation.

Initially the assessment should be attempted with individual children or in a small group situation (not more than four children to a group). You need to be absolutely clear that your role is one of observer and prompt. The habit of teaching and guiding is ingrained in teachers, but must be set aside if you are to assess the child's present level of understanding effectively.

Once you are familiar with the check-ups it will be possible to carry out the assessment in the normal course of children's learning. Working with a small group of children is beneficial in that it is more relaxed than the one-to-one situation, and it is easier to stimulate a flow of discussion which will provide the basis of your assessment.

Focus on one specific aspect of understanding in the concept of area. Suppose you want to know if the children within your small group can compare the area of two 2-D shapes by using non-standard units.
● Prepare two card shapes so that it is not clear which has the greater area.
● Present the children with a selection of identical tiles (triangular, square, circular) and a set of non-identical tiles.
● Ask them to find out whether the two shapes cover the same amount of space or a different amount of space.

Practical testing should take place initially with small groups to create a relaxed atmosphere.

This is essentially what you are looking for:

● Is the child using a regular unit to measure the shape?
● Does she appreciate that the same unit must be used to cover both shapes?
● Does she see the need for shapes which tessellate (leaving no gaps)?
● Can she see that the areas can be compared by comparing the two numbers?

Listen to the children's discussion during the task to make a fair assessment of their understanding of these ideas. Are they convinced by their own findings? A child may 'successfully' complete the task, then remark: 'I still think that the triangle covers the most space.'

One common problem with this process is that children assume that a probing question implies that the answer they have given is incorrect. (This says a lot about the way we interact with children in the normal classroom situation.) It is necessary at the beginning to explain that you will be asking questions about the way they thought something out, but this doesn't mean that their answer is wrong.

Follow-up

This mode of assessment is, by nature, diagnostic. It will indicate where the child needs further help, or whether he is ready for the next stage of learning. As each assessment is made, the results and comments should be entered into your records indicating, if necessary, where further work is needed on the concept. The ILEA *Checkpoints* materials are particularly helpful in providing pointers and suggestions for children who need further help.

The discussion which takes place naturally during an activity helps you to assess progress.

Assessing problem solving and investigations

Objectives

To assess the pupil's ability to approach problems.

In the previous section we looked at ways of assessing practical activities. These may take the form of problems to solve or mathematical investigations.

The essential target of the assessment will be the process which the child follows. The end product (ie the solution to the problem) is relatively unimportant, but if we can assess the child's ability to approach the problem, the information gained will give a clearer picture of the child's mathematical ability.

Level of development

Informal assessment can be used from the very early stages. You will base the child's introduction to problem solving on your judgement of their readiness.

Classroom organisation

Problem solving brings together children's knowledge of facts and concepts, with the skills they have acquired.

To attempt to assess their ability in the form of a checklist would be to devalue this activity and reduce it to a meaningless level. We need to assess the way in which the child approaches the problem and to evaluate the strategies used. This again must be achieved through a formative evaluation process: that is to say we need

● to observe the child in his attempts to tackle the problem,

● to ask for explanations of his approach.

There is no correct or best method to solve a problem. Investigations are essentially open-ended and allow children to work at their own level. When you watch a mixed ability group of children working at an investigation, you will see many different approaches: one child may be working by trial and error, whilst another might see through the problem quickly and apply a more systematic method. This might take the form of

- reducing the problem to a smaller one,
- using knowledge of a similar problem,
- 'holding' one variable whilst investigating another.

While the children work, try to ascertain where difficulties are arising. The following questions may help:

- Has the child the confidence and self-assurance needed to tackle the question?
- Is she able to draw on mathematical facts and patterns which help her to understand the problem?
- Is she able to apply appropriate strategies to the problem?

The first question is concerned with the pupil's attitude. If this appears to be negative, indicated by a lack of interest or involvement, you must decide whether the

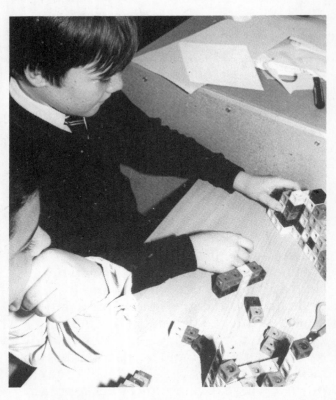

A mixed ability group will adopt various approaches.

activity is appropriate. Does it demand skills and concepts beyond her grasp? Is it difficult to get into? Ideally, problems and investigations should be based on practical activities so that there is some aspect of the problem which can be approached while the

children mull over the next stage. Time is also a very important factor. When adults are faced with a problem, we do not expect to come up with an immediate answer, so children must be allowed time to reflect on a problem and turn it over in their mind.

If a child is to draw on skills and concepts already acquired, then these must be firmly established. So the problem should be at a level where most of the knowledge required is already assimilated. For instance, if the investigation leads to the pattern of triangular numbers, it is not essential that the child has already studied these, but he should have met some work in which number patterns were investigated.

Pose a problem to a small group of children. For example: take a cube made from 27 smaller cubes (Dienes MAB materials or Multilink cubes could be used). Ask the children to imagine that we are going to paint each surface of the 3×3 cube. The smaller cubes will receive varying amounts of paint: some will be painted on three faces, some on two faces, some on one face, and some not at all. Can the children discover how many faces will be painted on each cube?

Part of the problem here is in organising the solution and children should be encouraged to try their own methods of organisation. By providing a structure for them, the teacher is imposing or recommending a method of solution. Previous knowledge of the properties of a cube is useful, but not essential, as the problem can be answered by visualisation and counting.

When the problem is expanded to ask the same question about different sized cubes, the need for a system becomes more apparent, and the geometric knowledge becomes more important.

You need to answer the following questions:

- Does the child understand the problem?
- Is he able to analyse visually the 3×3 cube?
- Is he able to organise his results?
- Is he using a systematic approach (eg checking by totalling the number of cubes)?
- Is he able to explain verbally what he does?

In secondary schools, profiling has become an important means of giving a more complete picture of what a child can do. This involves asking the child to comment on his own progress. In the area of investigations this is a particularly useful innovation, and one which may transfer well to the primary situation. The information provided will probably not help to grade the work, but should help the teacher to evaluate some aspects of the learning process. The stage of reflection should also help the child to see himself as an active learner in control of that learning process, and as a valued individual capable of contributing to the assessment procedure.

With the increased use of problem solving in schools, children should become more *au fait* with problem solving strategies. It is debatable, however, whether these should be taught in the same way that other methods are taught. It would be more appropriate perhaps for children to become aware of different strategies and to be able to select and use appropriate ones as and when they are needed.

A cube investigation was used to assess progress.

Formulating a school plan

Objectives

To formulate a system, through discussion, which will work in its own given circumstances, and which is useful and appropriate to the school situation.

Although the testing procedures should not lead the curriculum (ie you should not be beguiled into teaching to the tests), an effective overall plan should enhance the curriculum and reflect the width and scope of the school's work.

Level of development

The school plan should encompass all levels within the school and provide continuity with feeder schools and those into which it feeds.

Classroom organisation

The purposes of assessment might be to
● evaluate a child's understanding of a particular topic,
● make a comparison between children in a group,
● ascertain the teacher's effectiveness in teaching a particular topic,
● assist in placing children in ability groups,
● monitor the teaching and learning over a period of time.

The findings from the assessment may then be used for different purposes:
● to plan learning experiences for a particular child,
● to provide feedback, from which further plans can develop,
● to place children in groups of similar ability,
● to indicate areas of success and concern for further school development.

Assessment should mirror the learning process and take into account the aims of the curriculum. It is only worth while when carried out with a clear purpose in mind and when it is appropriate for the style of teaching.

Unfortunately, certain aspects of mathematics, such as the learning of facts and acquisition of skills, are much easier to assess than others. This can lead to an unbalanced situation in which methods are devised which test some sections, with little attention paid to others, so that the quality of the teaching and learning situation is not reflected in the findings of the assessment. An even greater danger is that you will

102

eventually concentrate solely on the areas which are tested.

For many years assessment has taken the form of written tests of skills and facts. But these are only a limited part of maths learning, and if they are the only areas assessed, they could assume a false importance in the minds of teachers, pupils and parents. The most commonly used standardised tests concentrate on these aspects alone, and teachers and parents must be aware of this when the results of such tests are used to make major decisions in the academic life of their children.

In order to develop a school policy it is necessary to decide
● why assessment is required,
● what needs to be assessed,

Allow children to select strategies in problem solving.

● how to do this,
● what kind of records would be useful,
● who would use them.

It must be clearly understood how records are to be used before a system is developed. Any system should incorporate as its priorities
● simplicity in recording,
● ease of access to the information contained.

The Cockcroft Committee were told by some secondary school teachers that they took little or no notice of information received from their feeder schools, as they wished to give the children a fresh start. The report of the committee states: 'We cannot accept that it can be justifiable to ignore information provided by schools in which pupils may have spent as long as seven years.'

My own research into primary–secondary liaison revealed that one reason why primary school records were not used extensively was because the information was not easily accessible. The records were available to the staff, but were often produced in an idiosyncratic way which made the information difficult to read.

If a system is developed which works effectively within a school, and is used to convey information from one person to another within that school, then it is much easier to transfer to the staff of a different school.

Relying on the informal transfer of information from teacher to teacher has obvious drawbacks when someone leaves that school, but creating an effective record system has more to do with developing effective planning procedures as part of an overall assessment plan for the school.

Achieving a balance between what you want to assess and what records can realistically be kept, will provide the basis for a workable system.

Catering for individual children

Catering for individual children

INTRODUCTION

All teachers of mathematics will be aware of the need to provide meaningful material for both the more-able and the less-able pupil. It should be an integral part of their thinking that the needs of those children who have special talents or learning difficulties in this subject are catered for. The requirements of the more-able pupil may well be more complex than those of the slow-learner. The latter, while needing more easily accomplished steps towards learning and reinforcing a mathematical idea, will probably still be struggling with the concept, while the

more-able child will have long since moved on to more difficult problems.

The less-able child will normally be working well within the framework of the mathematics planned for his particular age group or class; he will, of course, need plenty of games, examples and 'fun' exercises to help him accomplish his learning but, nevertheless, all this will normally come within the limits of what his teacher has planned.

Satisfying the needs of the more-able child will, however, prove much more taxing for the teacher. It is all too easy to push the more-able children on to the next level, to a set of more difficult problems, or even into work normally aimed at older children. Whilst the child may cope, and may progress quite well, his learning will eventually become narrow, and he will not be using and reinforcing concepts already learned along the way. He will soon get bored and frustrated, and will grow to resent being given extra work to do, if it is not interesting and challenging. Material should be provided which will demand the use of concepts already established, giving lateral extension to the child's learning. Activities for both types of children should be stimulating, and many of them should be related to the interests and experiences of the children. Many sports, such as football, can be used for mathematical problems. Look at, for example, 'angles' in football; the idea of a goalkeeper 'narrowing the angle'; the trajectory of the ball. Developing tasks related to topics included in your mathematics curriculum can be a difficult and time-consuming activity.

To fit the practical needs of most teachers, these should take up as little of the teacher's time as possible – the remainder of the class will (quite rightly) be demanding the lion's share of their teachers' attention, and extension activities should not be the source of distraction or undue allocation of time.

Materials involved should ideally be those normally found in the classroom, and specialised apparatus or equipment should be avoided. Children should know where to find things and be able to settle down quickly to their assignments. Many of these may involve children working in twos or threes, and sharing the organisation and problem solving.

Games and challenges for the less-able child may involve classmates helping, or joining in the activity. Time should be allowed for discussion, and explanation of what has been accomplished by the children on a child-to-child, child-to-group (or class) and child-to-teacher basis. The emphasis should be on enjoyment, investigation and discovery. Activities need not only be of a practical nature and may well include number puzzles, statistics, data work, symmetry, calculators tasks and a whole host of other interest-related ideas.

Children must know where to find materials for extension work to enable them to settle down quickly.

Objectives

The general aims for those working with children who have special needs in mathematics must be to cater as fully as possible for the needs of each individual, and to provide as much learning as is required, while providing interest, challenges and fun for the child.

The objectives, which are the stepping-stones towards these aims, must therefore include:
- a careful examination of the core topics taught to a particular age group, and extensions or intermediate activities

- to match each task to the individual child. A child may not need to complete a whole card or assignment. Perhaps only part of it may be relevant. Teachers may require a ten minute slot to be filled – alternatively, an activity may develop into several lessons' work. Enthusiasm may wane, or children may be so interested that they seek further time. Flexibility is the key. Some children may have specific problems or abilities in certain areas of mathematics, and may need further activities relating to those areas only – for example, in number work. Children differ in their needs, and these will have to

Children may need further activities due to particular problems or abilities in certain areas.

planned so that they follow on or fit in as well as possible with the child's work.
- a careful consideration of the best means available to provide extension material. This may mean adopting some of the ideas and exercises in the excellently produced materials originating in the local authorities – many written by teachers for use by teachers; it may perhaps mean use of an individualised scheme like KMP or SMP, where the cards and tape cassette lessons can be given to individuals to fit in with the mainstream mathematics scheme.

be identified.
- to seek to provide activities tailored to the child's intellectual level, however high that may be. Some activities may provide difficulties for the teachers themselves. This is not unusual, especially when dealing with very able pupils, and teachers – especially those who are themselves not maths specialists – should not be afraid of embarking upon exercises in which they themselves may end up investigating with, or learning from, the pupils.

Level of development

Children of all ages may possess considerable ability in mathematics, and extension activities will have an important place in the consolidation of concepts and ideas for any age of child.

Children of the eleven and twelve year age group are often those in greatest need of additional material. Many at this stage are quite skilful in reading, performing and recording, and may finish set work very quickly. Equally, those children with difficulties may often be losing heart at this

Able mathematicians may not be fluent readers.

age, as their problems become more obvious, and they too need assignments in which they can succeed.

Reading ability is an important factor to consider. The child who is blessed with mathematical skill may not be a good reader, and language will have to be greatly simplified, or assignments could even be put on to tape. Poor reading ability is more likely to be the case with children who have difficulties in mathematics, and much interest can be added to work for the less-

able child if a set of cassettes are made especially for reinforcement activities. Hints, and even answers, can be included in the recordings to help the child achieve his goal.

Classroom organisation

Extension activities may require some specialised equipment, but most should involve materials readily available in the classroom. Paper (including a variety of squared paper, isometric, dotty etc), glue sticks, pins, paper fasteners, scissors, and practical equipment for weighing, measuring length, capacity, displacement by volume, and so on, should be easily accessible. Much can be improvised; for example, hinged desk lids and doors can be used to create slopes, or corners for children to investigate amounts of turning. Valuable teacher time can be saved if children are familiar with the storage areas and access to materials including practical and audio-visual equipment.

Materials and equipment should be easily accessible.

109

Plotting points from digit chain

This task may follow work done by children who have learned about the use of ordered pairs, and plotting points on a grid, or chains of numbers. The task involves completing chains of digits following a certain rule, and from the digits, forming ordered pairs of numbers to plot on a grid. Joining the points in order provides interesting patterns. There are many questions to be answered along the way!

Look at this number chain:

$$3\rightarrow12\rightarrow9\rightarrow36\rightarrow27\rightarrow$$

To find the next number, you must look carefully at the previous number and: multiply the units digit by 4 *then* add on the tens digit (if there is one)

So the number after 27 will be
$7 \times 4 = 28$
add $2\rightarrow30$
Continue the chain; what do you find?

Make ordered pairs from these numbers by:
- pairing each number with its following number

and
- pairing each number with itself.

So you will get
(3,12)
(12,12)
(12, 9)
(9, 9)
(9,36)
Complete this list.

Plot all the points on squared paper.
Join them up in order.
Label the axes of your grid in 3's.
Join the last point to the first.
What do you find?

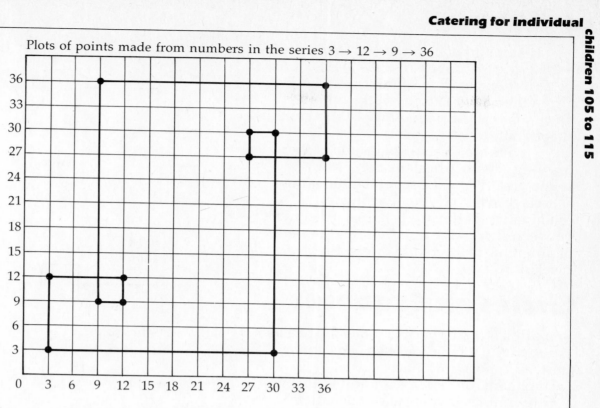

Plots of points made from numbers in the series 3 → 12 → 9 → 36

Try the exercise with another chain:
6→24→18→33→
What do you find?

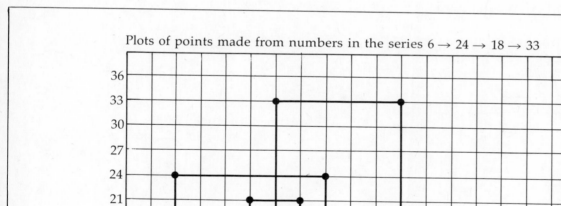

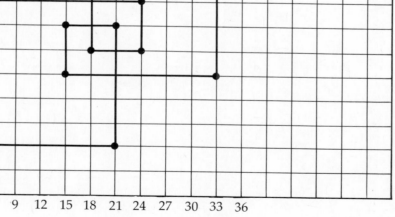

Plots of points made from numbers in the series 6 → 24 → 18 → 33

Try a number chain of your own. Start it with a single number. Investigate the grid patterns you get from different chains. Do any of them look like any of the others? Trace some of them if you wish, and cut the shapes out.

Results are fascinating. Some of the drawings are identical to others in size/shape/area. There are several interesting aspects of symmetry to investigate: examination of the digit chains, differences between successive numbers, and patterns of differences all provide interesting revelations.

Circles and squares

Since this is a number-orientated exercise, it is an activity which could be used at any time, as a short time-filler or as a springboard for looking at number puzzles. Later examples involve use of negative numbers, but the examples could be varied to suit younger children.

Some pupils may complete the puzzles but may fail to see any patterns or reasoning. Ask them to add up the numbers in the squares and compare results.

If you add the numbers in the circles, you will get the number in the square.

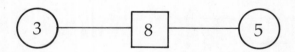

Try this one . . .

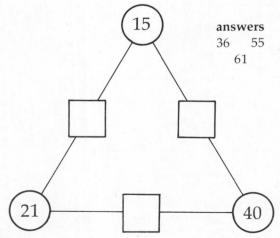

answers
36   55
    61

and this one . . .

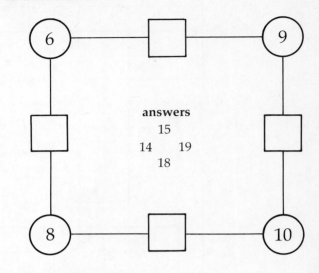

answers
15
14   19
    18

Easy? Try this one.

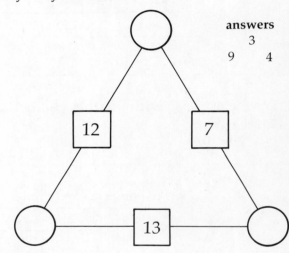

answers
3
9   4

Slightly more difficult!

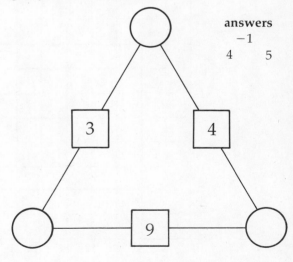

answers
−1
4   5

Can you find a method that works each time? Might some be impossible?

112

Let's look at some more patterns.

Can you make a rule which will tell you if there is an answer?

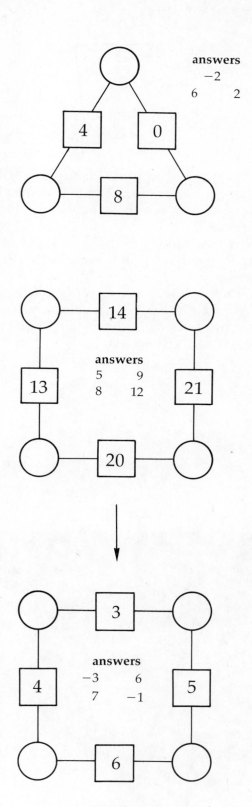

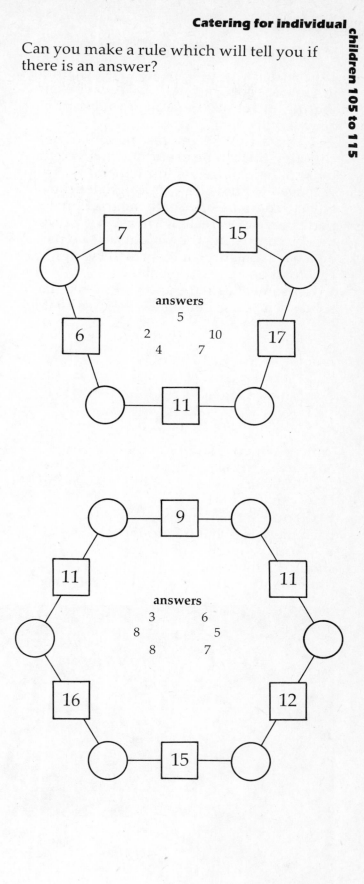

Practical fractions

The use of fractions appears to be declining in some schools, but practical concepts of sharing and equal division are still part of our everyday lives.

   This activity is interesting for younger children, but can be usefully employed for those older children of limited ability. They will need to know how to weigh, for they have to compare or equate the fractional parts they have created. They can achieve this by comparing the weights of two parts on a beam balance, or by actually weighing each part on a pressure balance.

● Get some Plasticine and make a regular solid such as a sphere or a cube. Use a table

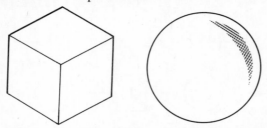

knife to cut your solid into two pieces of equal weight, as near as you can judge.

   Are you sure your two pieces are equal? How can you find out?

● Complete this sentence:

Each piece is (what fraction?) of the solid.

● Which properties of the two pieces should be the same?

(Investigate colour, shape, size, weight)

● Make the Plasticine into an irregular solid and repeat the exercise. How successful were you this time?

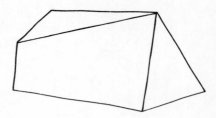

● Make six different solids, both regular and irregular. Try to cut each one into two equal pieces. Organise a way of recording your results.

● Now try making some solids and cut them into three equal pieces. What do you discover?

● Which solids are easiest to cut accurately?

● Experiment with other solids, cutting them into four, or perhaps five, equal pieces. Ask a friend to try.

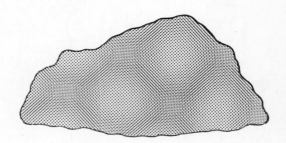

Shapes moulded from Plasticine were cut into two, then weighed to find out if they were equally divided.

Follow-up

Follow-up activities will be necessary in many of the tasks designed for the more-able child. Investigations may go on and on, and become more complex and detailed. Whilst the children's enthusiasm is there, they will be more than eager to look further into a topic. In some activities, it can be useful to include a 'sting in the tail' – a particularly difficult question which will really tax the able pupil and perhaps only be accomplished by the gifted.

Often, however, extension activities need to be kept short, perhaps while the rest of the class complete a section of work from the mainstream syllabus. This can mean that investigations may be limited to a single lesson, or at best two periods, until the teacher is ready to take the whole group on to further work or a new topic.

Follow-up activities for the less-able are somewhat easier to plan. If a previous activity has failed to establish or clarify a concept, then other parallel methods will have to be found. If an activity has been successfully completed, the pupil may again return to mainstream work, or may progress to a carefully selected but more demanding activity.

Involving parents

Involving parents

INTRODUCTION

OCTOPUS PUBLISHING

Over the last few years, the idea that teachers should be determined to involve parents in their children's reading has become accepted as good primary practice. Studies from Haringey, Coventry, Bristol, Bradford and Hackney have demonstrated how children's progress can be improved by encouraging sustained parental participation in this area.

However, in maths the situation is very different. Mathematics, it is said, differs from reading in several important ways.

Many parents have always helped their children by reading to and with them, but often they do not believe themselves competent to offer comparable help in mathematics.

The *Cockcroft Report* reminds us that parents can exert undue or inappropriate pressure in mathematics. Some also have a traditional and narrow view of the subject, stemming from their own experiences of maths at school.

Parents sometimes find the maths they see in the classroom rather confusing. It doesn't seem much like the maths they did themselves, and it can be difficult to see the point of what has been done.

Teachers can be much less confident in maths, too, and they may see the idea of involving parents as threatening rather than helpful.

Teachers, parents and children may see maths as a dull subject in which extra work is given out as a punishment rather than being considered a pleasure.

However, there is now evidence that parental involvement can play the same positive role in mathematics as it does in reading. IMPACT (Maths for Parents, Children and Teachers), a scheme which mirrors the PACT reading initiatives, was started in 1985 in a number of inner-city schools. It has shown that it is possible to involve parents in maths without a retrogressive effect on the curriculum. In fact, parental participation in this area has improved classroom practice and engendered a more confident and positive attitude towards mathematics on the part of the teachers, parents and the children involved.

The reasons for approaching the subject as we do become much clearer to the parents, too, and when they can see granny's handspan and the baby's head circumference on the wall along with others, the maths ceases to be so intimidating and becomes quite familiar!

The children will explain mathematical activities to their parents, and simply putting into words what they have been doing at school helps them to clarify some of the ideas. They will also be doing mathematical tasks normally confined to the classroom, and making links between maths in everyday life and what they do at school.

BRADLEY MOLE

Organisation

Because there has not been as much research into parental involvement in mathematics as there has been in the area of language, there is no model for the best way to go about it. It is best to adopt a number of strategies and be prepared to adapt and be flexible.

Initial parents meetings

It is very important to speak to all the parents involved. You may need to hold two or even three meetings at different times:

119

one at school-starting time, one at school-finishing time, and one evening meeting. Some schools involving parents in their children's reading adopted a policy of home visiting if they failed to persuade parents to come to meetings. The same could be done in this case.

It is often possible to speak to the majority of the parents in the initial two or three meetings, and then to see the remaining parents by arranging to meet them individually. This sounds like a lot of work, but two short meetings at the beginning and end of the day, plus a few words with a small number of individual parents on a couple of subsequent mornings or afternoons, will suffice.

Reporting back

To ensure that parental participation *is* participation and not simply a means of getting children to do homework, it is essential that a dialogue is maintained. It may be helpful to adopt the same system used for parental involvement in children's reading. For example, if the parents record their responses in a small book or on report cards, these can also be used for their comments about the maths done at home. Alternatively, 'comment sheets' can be sent home for both parents and children to use.

Follow-up meetings

It is important to hold a series of meetings – short and frequent rather than long and seldom – in which the work being done at home and in the classroom is discussed. It is in everyone's interest to pool information since the parents are seeing a side of the children's maths learning which the teacher does not see, and vice versa. Also, it is important to maintain regular lines of communication in case there is any confusion or worry about the best way to assist a child in a specific situation.

Regular chats

Perhaps the most effective way of developing and sustaining a dialogue with parents is those chats first thing in the morning or last thing in the afternoon, when parents and teachers have a few minutes to share snippets of information. 'He just couldn't seem to get the hang of how to write the numbers above ten' or 'I told her not to count the numbers on both dice when adding them, but to count on from the larger number . . .' are the sort of remarks which are immensely valuable in terms of the child's work the next day.

Regular discussions between parents and teachers are very useful.

Starting point

The programme of meetings and activities may seem slightly daunting for some teachers, so it is best to begin gradually, taking one stage at a time.

Dominoes is a good game for your library.

Parent workshops

Try holding a series of parent workshops where parents are encouraged to come for a short time and join in. For example, the school can stay open from 4pm until 8pm and parents can either stay and have tea or drop in later in the evening to try out a few maths activities. It is even better if the children are there to show them how to do it.

Game libraries

A 'game library' in school, from which parents or children can borrow games, is a good starting point for maths activities at home. As well as including some commercial games, you, the children, and parents can make games to add to the library. The whole idea of inventing your own games can arise out of this.

Information books or pamphlets

Written information is usually the least effective way of involving parents, but it is better than nothing. As alternatives to the standard and rather intimidating booklets about the 'new maths', you could make a booklet of selected and appropriate activities or games for parents and children to do at home, or encourage the children to write their own small booklet about the maths they do in school using examples of their own work as illustrations.

Parental participation

There is no doubt that involving parents in their children's learning is helpful. It helps the children, the parents and the teachers. As Dorothy Hamilton says about parental involvement in reading: 'It does not in the end involve more work for the teachers, but rather it means working in a different way.' She also remarks: 'Parents already are helping their children at home.' It seems to me that, as teachers, we can either ignore this or embrace it. The evidence shows us that we do much better to embrace it.

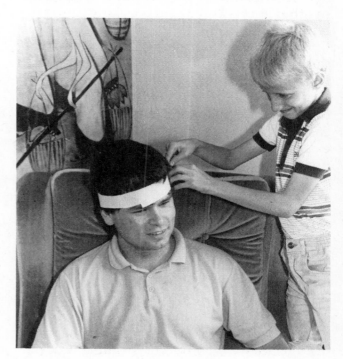

Involve parents as much as possible.

Work to go home

Parental participation immediately raises the question of what sort of maths can be done at home. Since the aim is to involve parents, it is very important that the activities do not look like homework, which tends to be an individual activity.

Home activities feed into and inform classwork, although they rarely fall into a neat mathematics category, but often bring in other subject areas such as language and art.

The evidence from IMPACT shows that the maximum success in terms of the number of parents and children taking part was achieved when home activities arose out of and fed back into classwork. The easiest way to illustrate this is with examples of the different types of material used.

Making or doing something

There are activities which can be done at home, although they would not be very practical in class because there are not enough adults to help each child.

Each of the following activities was used in such a way that it became the focal point of the week's classwork.

Make a container

These activities were (see page 147) sent home with reception and middle infants. In both cases, the children and parents produced between them some really imaginative and spectacular work which might not have been possible in class. See Fans and lanterns on page 148 for further ideas.

One child made an igloo, while another made a cone containing one piece of popcorn for every child in the class. Yet another drew and cut out a 'mother', ''cos mummies are containers for babies'.

With such a wealth of resources coming in, the subsequent week's classwork can be organised around them. Children wrote about their containers and then measured the capacity, which led on to further work.

Make a handspan

The children made their own handspans at home together with those of several members of their families, and used these to measure various objects in class (see pages 149 and 150).

Another activity led on from Make a handspan, with the need for a standard unit of measurement. Children took home the orange decimetre rods which form the 10-rods in Cuisinaire sets. All the children (top infants) drew themselves and their families on the squared paper provided. Although it was not made explicit, this activity involved the use of scale and proportion, two topics in mathematics which are usually reserved until much later. None of the children had trouble doing this activity at home, although once again it would have been impossible in class given the adult-pupil ratio.

Collecting information

These activities or tasks are also used to set up the week's work.

These activities feed into the classwork by enabling the child to bring information about life outside school into the classroom. This may take the form of drawings, objects or data, and can be used by the teacher either with the whole class or to develop each individual's work in this area.

Heavy potato

This activity (see page 151) was used to construct a week's work on weight. The children compared the weights of their potatoes using balances, and measured their sizes in various directions. Throughout the week the children continued their search for ever larger and larger potatoes; one child was even suspected of having surreptitiously sliced a bit off the end of a rival potato!

Time spiral

This arose out of classwork involving a similar spiral which the children were putting up on the wall. They were doing quite a bit of work on time, and the year spiral was intended to help them with their computations. In doing the spirals at home, the children found out about a number of events which were then fitted into the class spiral. They also used the spiral to work out how old they would be in 20 years time and wrote about what they would look and be like. See photocopiable pages 152 and 153.

Floating and sinking

This was partly a data collecting enterprise, but also a 'making and doing' activity. They were all highly motivated by the initial class discussion about whether it is possible to make a pin float. They collected information about the sorts of things which will and won't float and displayed this information on a Venn diagram, which made the subsequent week's task of collating the

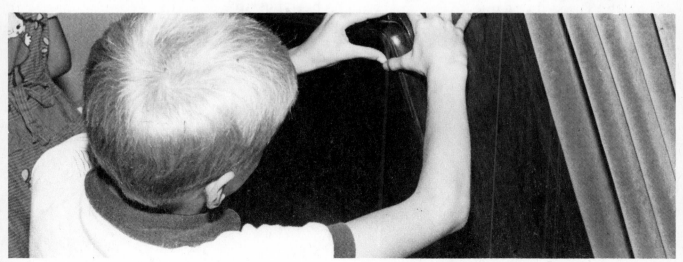

Using handspans to measure different objects is an ideal project to do at home.

information on to a class diagram relatively simple. See photocopiable pages 154 and 155.

Games, puzzles and investigations

There was some indication from IMPACT that this type of activity was not as popular as the first two. This could be because of the implication: 'You play the games at home and we'll do the 'serious' maths in school.' Although maths advisers and most maths teachers recognise the importance and usefulness of games in mathematics, they may be quite differently perceived by parents.

Activities in this category were successful only if they arose out of the classwork and fed back into it. It is sometimes tempting to 'graft' a game on to the classwork, but this does nothing to inspire the children or their parents to play it at home. Investigations can be successful only if the parents know their purpose.

Three-dice
See also Multiplying grid on pages 159 and 160.

Both games involve what used to be called 'skills practice'. This can be done very effectively as part of a game since it is much less tedious and there is usually an incentive to get it right. See pages 156 and 157 for the Three-dice game.

The children work out 50 or so sums in their heads in less than half an hour. Since they are keen to finish the sums quickly, they tend to improve their methods and speed up the process. Some children and parents dislike competitive games, so point out that games like these can be played non-competitively against oneself, the clock or even a teddy bear.

Box investigation
This arose out of work on solid shapes (see page 158). The children had been asked to look at different shaped boxes and to select one to bring in to school, where they cut open the boxes to find out what their nets looked like. At home they all constructed a cube using a standard arrangement of six squares. This led to the construction of cubes and cuboids in class, which in turn led to the Box investigation. Because this was so much a part of the classwork, it was extremely popular with both the children and the parents at home. In such circumstances an open-ended and investigational activity can prove stimulating and enlivening, rather than bewildering and somewhat threatening to parents.

Some of these activities have been produced by Julia Griffiths, Sally Wilson and Kate Frood. Without their help, and that of the rest of the staff of Fleet School, Kentish Town, London IMPACT would not have been possible.

Squared paper (centimetre squares), see page 27

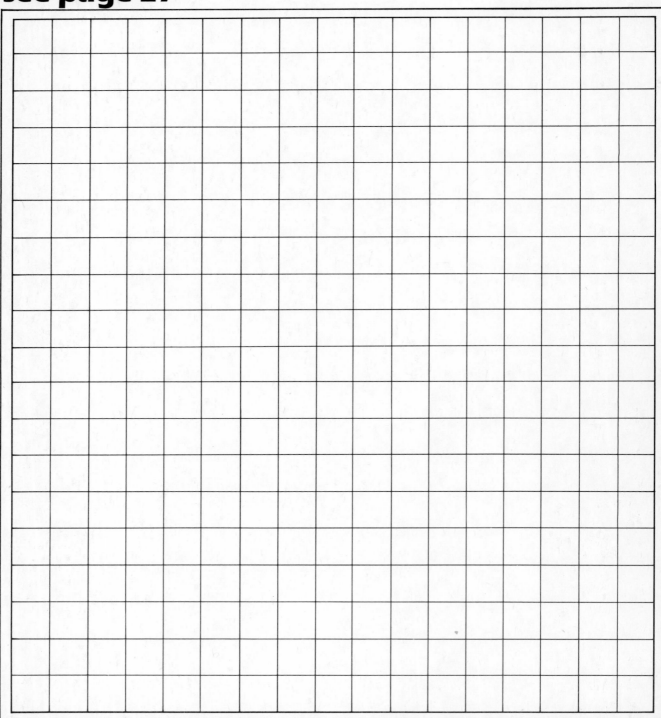

Dotty paper (squares), see page 27

Dotty paper (triangles), see page 27

Flags, see pages 30 and 31

Flags, see pages 30 and 31

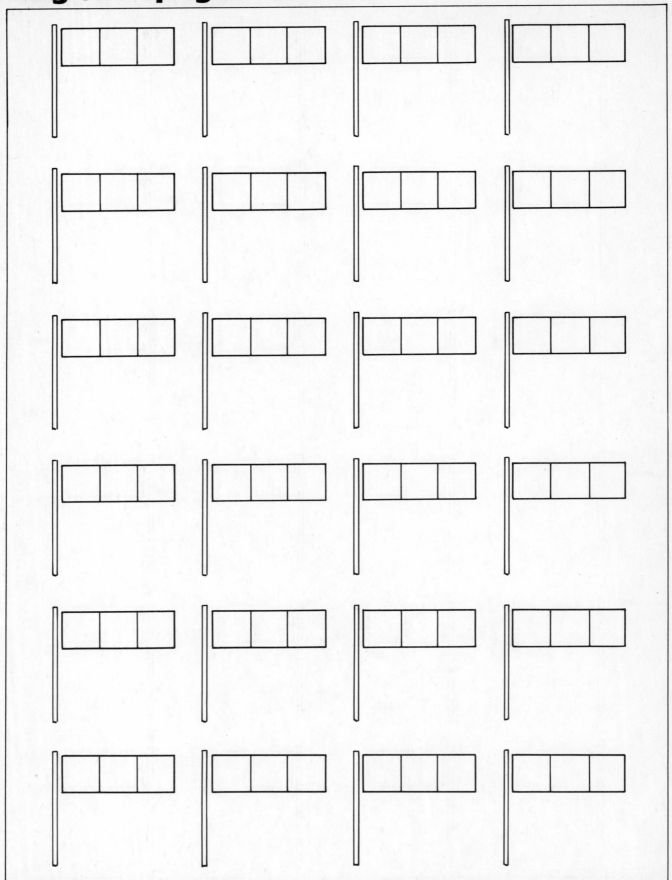

Flags, see pages 30 and 31

Flags, see pages 30 and 31

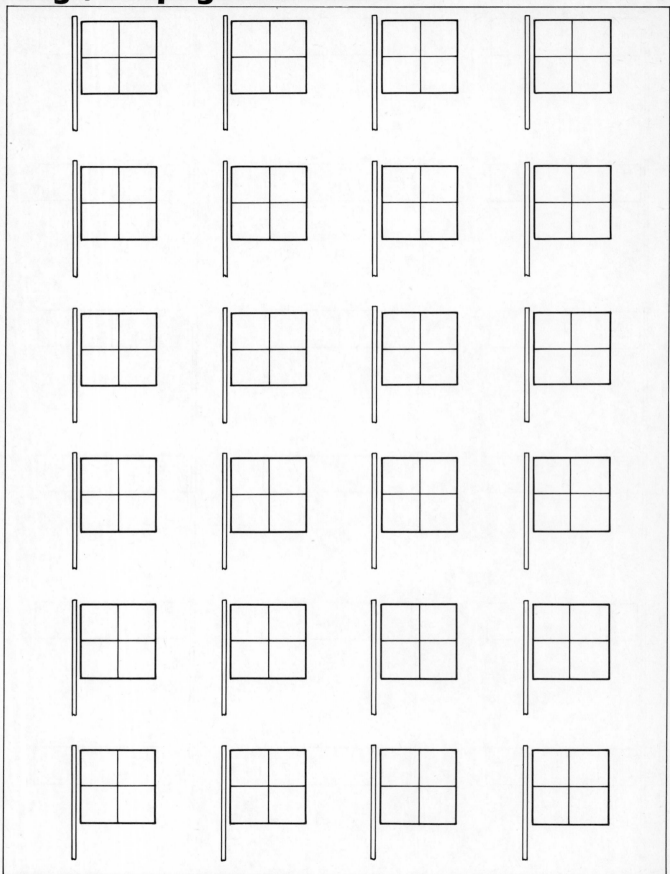

Flags, see pages 30 and 31

Flags, see pages 30 and 31

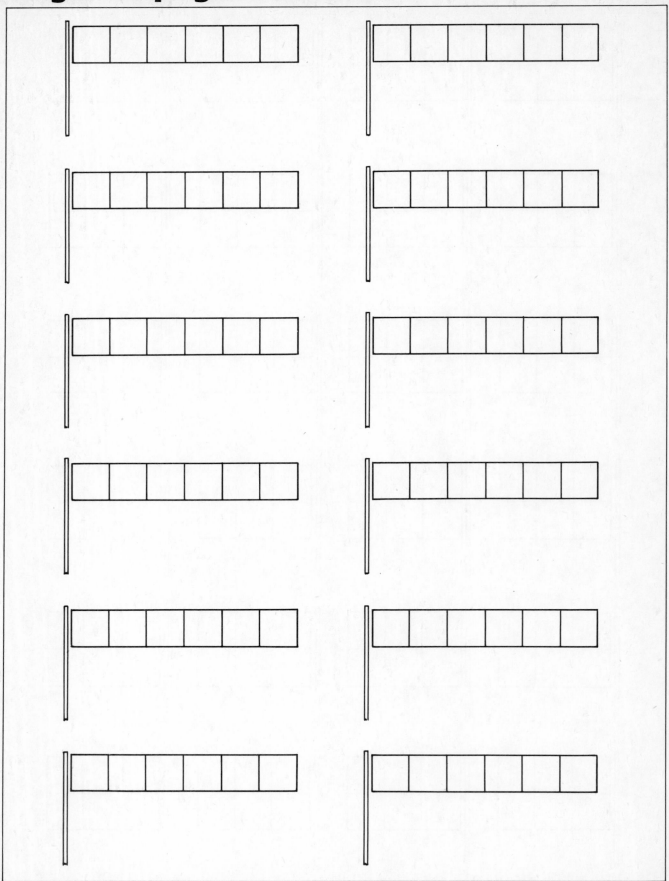

Isometric pattern, see page 36

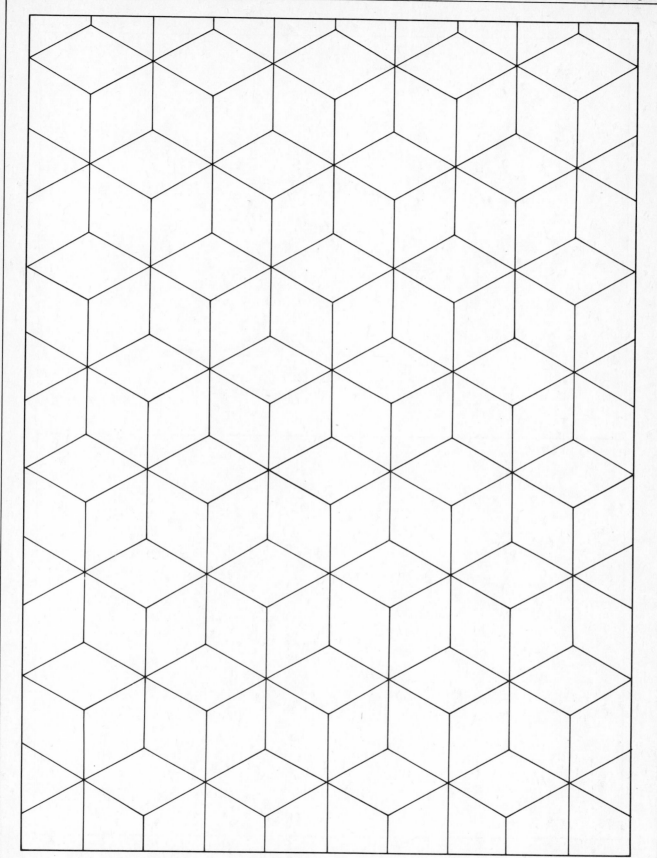

Carroll diagram, see page 60

Carroll diagram, see page 60

Venn diagram, see page 60

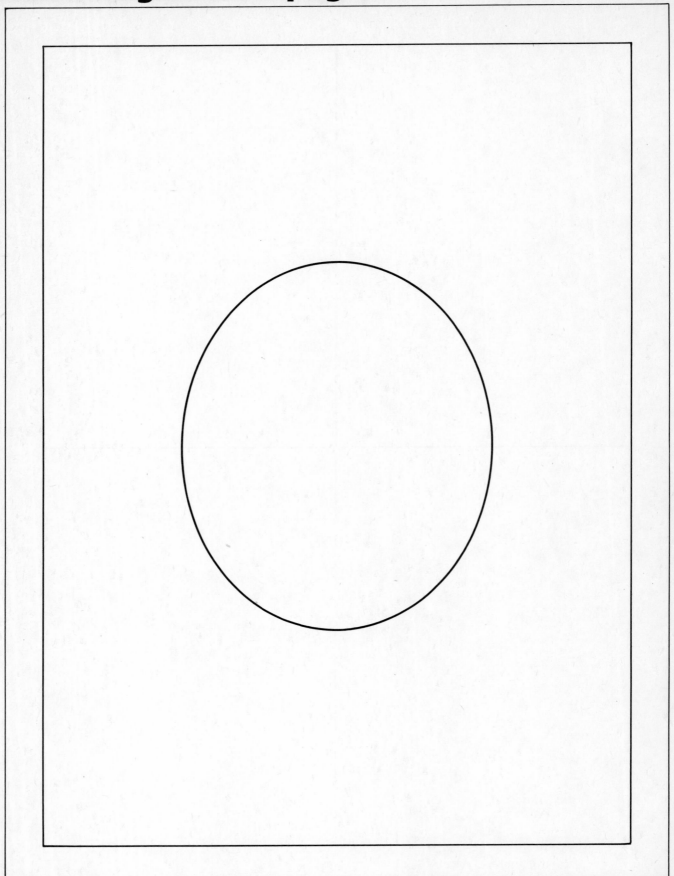

Grid, see page 60

Grid, see page 60

Grid, see page 60

Forecast and check, see page 76

Number	Operation	Forecast	Check

Bullseye, see page 78

Start number	Estimate	Calculator answer

Touchdown, see page 79

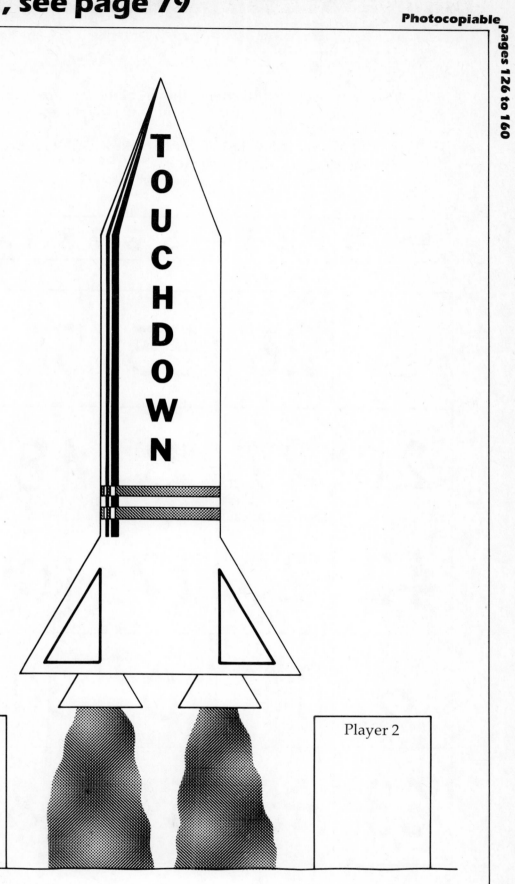

Four in a row, see page 81

You may use any of the keys shown in the key box to try and make the numbers in the square. If you make the number you can cover it with one of your counters.

The winner is the first player to make a row of four counters of the same colour in any direction.

Key	0 1 2 3 4 5 6 7 8 9 × =	Box

2	26	35	56	18
21	27	8	48	40
42	20	17	10	32
6	14	0	30	24
63	45	54	28	12

Containers

Make a container of any shape from some or all of the card. You can cut, stick, fold, clip, etc as is necessary.

Fans and Lanterns

I'm sure you would like to help your child construct either a fan or a lantern.

These can be any shape. Please cut, stick, fold and design at your own free will. Discussion is very important.

Your child could estimate the number of patterns it is possible to use, the number of cuts, folds, etc. They could then count the actual number used.

Finally I would be grateful if, when your child brings the finished product to school, they could explain to a friend how it was made.

Good Luck!

Handspans

This week we would like you to make your child's handspan and also that of any other person in the house. Here's how........
Cut out a strip of paper about 3cm or 1in wide.

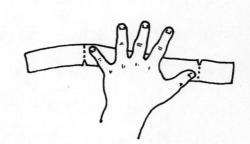

Lay the child's hand across the strip, stretching the fingers as wide as possible.
Cut the strip so that it is exactly the length of the outstretched hand.
The child now writes their name on the strip and decorates it nicely.

◆◆◆TOBY◆◆◆

Repeat this process for anyone else in the family; brother, sister, baby, daddy, granny.

Now bring your handspans to school.

Measuring with decimetres

10 centimetres = 1 decimetre

10 decimetres = 1 metre

Use a decimetre strip to measure someone in your house. Be very careful to be accurate. Try to guess first! Then cut one of the strips of squared paper to represent their height using 1 square to every 1 decimetre. Eg If Mum measured 16 decimetres, cut your strip 16 squares long. Then draw your person in their strip making sure that their head is at the top of the paper and their feet touch the bottom. This will represent their true height.

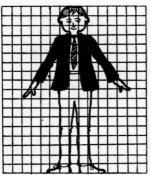

18 decimetres
so 18 squares

You may like to do a little person you know too or do yourself again.

8 and a bit decimetres so 8 and a bit squares

* The children have all done this for themselves in * class. This activity not only practises using a standard unit of measurement but shows how accurate comparisons can then be made. Eg The * tallest parent should have the tallest drawing. * Do help your child to measure as accurately as possible. Please bring your pictures to school for a family portrait!

Heavy Potato

Bring in the heaviest potato you can find. Fill in as many names as you can on the diagram below.

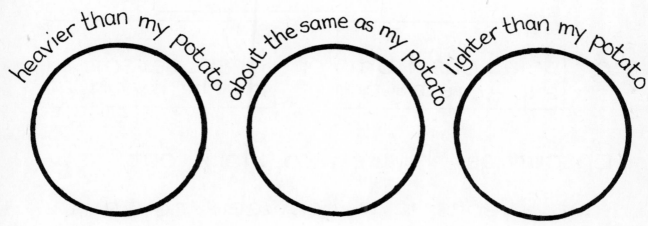

heavier than my potato

about the same as my potato

lighter than my potato

Hint to parents
Select some things to write on this diagram that we can check in school, for example: a sock, a shoe, a pencil...

Time Spiral

The time spiral attached is marked with the years from 1959 to 1990. Can you mark on the spiral any dates of family, community or general interest.

For example, | 1978 Annie was born.

or | 1981 Relations from India came to stay. | or | 1969 First person on the moon.

Encourage children to work out how many years it is between certain events. For example, "I was born 10 years after the first man landed on the moon." Colour the spiral in and bring it into school.

Time spiral, see page 123

| 1981 | 1980 | 1979 | 1978 | 1977 |

| 1982 | | | | 1976 |

| 1983 | 1966 | 1965 | 1964 | 1975 |

| 1983 | 1967 | | 1963 | 1975 |

| | | 1959 | | |

| 1984 | 1968 | 1960 | 1962 | 1974 |

| | | 1961 | | |

| 1985 | 1969 | | | 1973 |

| | 1970 | 1971 | 1972 | |

| 1986 | | | | |

| 1987 | 1988 | 1989 | 1990 | |

153

Float or sink

1 Ask your child to predict whether or not something will float.

2 Try getting things which do not usually float to do so.
For example, you can get a pin to float by putting it on tissue paper (a paper hankie). This then sinks leaving the pin to float.

3 Try to make a floating object sink by adding weights.

4 Try making a paper ship! (or a ship made from something else!)

Float or sink

Can you help your child draw or write the things they find in these sets.

Will float

float first and then sink

sink

Three dice game

Throw 3 dice and add up the numbers thrown. Cover the total <u>wherever</u> it appears on the board.

You could also try "Wild throw" ie: If any 2 of your dice add up to 10, you may choose a number and cover all instances of that number on the board. The winner is the first person to cover a line.

In both games, the children are recognising and searching out different numbers, practising number bonds to 10, and addition. The children can be encouraged to count on from the largest number in order to add up eg 5 + 6 + 3 can be performed 7, 8, 9, 10, 11, and then 12, 13, 14.

Sometimes it is hard for the children to see which numbers are the most useful ones to cover on a wild throw ie those least likely or impossible to obtain using three dice only.

Watching out for the pairs of numbers which add up to ten is a very effective way of getting children to remember their number bonds.

Three dice, see page 124

10	14	4	10	12	13	10	10	20	7
10	1	15	14	12	6	20	4	10	7
11	12	18	11	7	8	12	11	6	7
9	5	10	12	12	8	8	10	12	14
18	6	18	3	14	15	12	5	11	19
13	15	10	13	3	11	10	19	13	11
4	17	2	15	13	3	11	1	8	16
16	12	14	12	14	12	6	10	12	8
9	9	9	9	9	9	9	19	20	16
16	12	12	17	17	2	12	14	5	13

Box investigations

The usual arrangement of 6 squares that will fold to make up a cube is this one:

Which other arrangements of 6 squares will work?

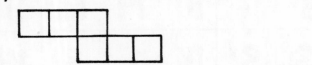

Will this one?   or this one?

Try out others on the squared paper.

The process of investigating in mathematics is an immensely useful one. The children are encouraged to develop logical thought processes – hypothesising, predicting, testing their predictions and demonstrating their discoveries so that someone else can understand them. The more investigations they do, the better will be their grasp of the processes involved in mathematics.

Multiplication grid game

Throw 2 dice.
Multiply the totals.
You may place a counter on that number on your grid. Then let your opponent have a turn. They must use different coloured counters.

The winner is the first person to get 4 counters next to each other in a row in any direction.

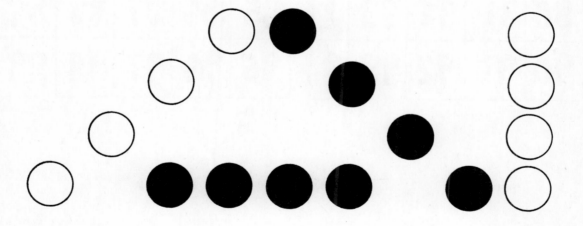

Multiplication grid game, see page 124

0	1	2	3	4	5	6	7	8	9
10	11	12	13	14	15	16	17	18	19
20	21	22	23	24	25	26	27	28	29
30	31	32	33	34	35	36	37	38	39
40	41	42	43	44	45	46	47	48	49
50	51	52	53	54	55	56	57	58	59
60	61	62	63	64	65	66	67	68	69
70	71	72	73	74	75	76	77	78	79
80	81	82	83	84	85	86	87	88	89
90	91	92	93	94	95	96	97	98	99

Resources

Books

Better Schools: a Summary DES (HMSO 1985).

Calculator Mathematics K Tyler and H Burkhardt (Blackie 1982/83).

Calculators in the Primary School (PM 537) (Open University Press, Learning Materials Services, Centre for Continuing Education, Open University, PO Box 188, Milton Keynes).

Checkpoints (ILEA Learning Resources Branch, 275 Kennington Lane, London SE11 5QZ).

Children Learning Mathematics L Dickson, M Brown and O Gibson (Holt, Rinehart and Winston 1984).

Children's Understanding of Mathematics: 11–16 K Hart (John Murray 1981).

Electronic Calculators Nuffield Mathematics Group (Longman 1984).

Investigating Numbers Ed Catherall (Wayland 1982).

Investigating Shapes Ed Catherall (Wayland 1983).

Mathematical Activities Brian Bolt (CUP 1982).

Mathematics Counts: Report of the Committee of the Enquiry into the Teaching of Mathematics in Schools under the Chairmanship of Dr W H Cockcroft DES (HMSO 1982).

Mathematics 5–11 DES (HMSO 1979).

Mathematics 5–16 DES (HMSO 1985).

Notes on Mathematics for Children Association of Teachers of Maths (CUP 1977).

Nuffield Maths: Challengers series Eric Albany and Ray Bull (Longman 1986) *Book A* and *Book B*.

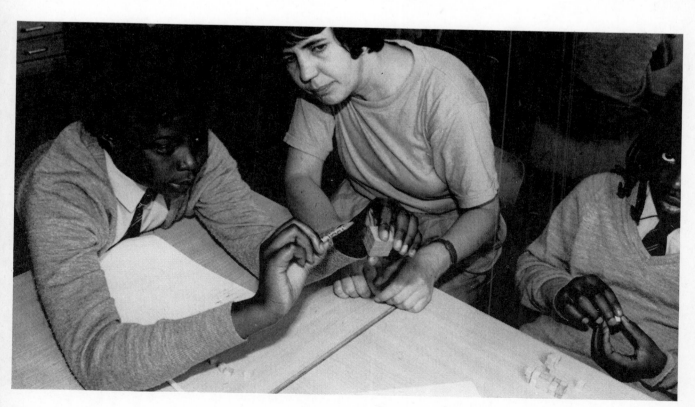

PACT Parents Teachers Children D Hamilton and A Griffiths (Methuen 1984).
Pointers (CUP 1984).
Primary Mathematics Today and Tomorrow Hilary Shuard (Longman 1986).
Primary Surveys 1, 2, 3 Assessment of Performance Unit (HMSO 1980–82).
Sources of Mathematical Discovery Lorraine Mottershead (Blackwell 1977).
Thinking Things Through Leone Burton (Blackwell 1984).
Working Notes on Assessment (Association of Teachers of Mathematics 1985).

Equipment suppliers

Suppliers' catalogues are available on request.

James Galt & Co Ltd
Brookfield Road
Cheadle
Cheshire
SK8 2PN
tel 061 428 8511

Hestair Hope Ltd
St Philips Drive, Royton
nr Oldham
Lancashire
OL2 6AG
tel 061 652 1411

Philip & Tacey Ltd
Customer Services Dept
North Way
Andover
Hants
SP10 5BA
tel 0264 332171
(Use headed note-paper when requesting catalogues.)

E J Arnold & Son Ltd
Parkside Lane
Dewsbury Road
Leeds
LS11 5TD
tel 0532 772112

Tarquin Publications
Stradbroke
Diss
Norfolk
IP21 5JP
tel 037 984 218

Cuisenaire Company,
11 Crown Street
Reading
RG1 2TQ
tel 0734 873101

Taskmaster Ltd
Morris Road
Leicester
LE2 6BR
tel 0533 704286

Nottingham Educational Supplies
17 Ludlow Hill Road
Melton Road
West Bridgford
Nottingham
NG2 6HD
tel 0602 397112

Sources for software

AUCBE
Chiltern Computing
Endymion Road
Hatfield
Hertfordshire
AL10 8AU

Cambridge Micro Software
Cambridge University Press
The Edinburgh Building
Shaftesbury Road
Cambridge
CB2 2RU

Cambridge Software House
The Town Hall
St Ives
Cambridgeshire

4Mation Educational Resources
Linden Lea
Rock Park
Barnstaple
Devon
EX32 9AQ

Ginn & Co Ltd
Prebendal House
Parson's Fee
Aylesbury
Buckinghamshire
HP20 2QX

Logotron Ltd
Dales Brewery
Guydir Street
Cambridge
CB1 2JL

Longman Micro Software
Longman Group UK Ltd
Longman House
Burnt Mill
Harlow
Essex
CM20 2JE

Microsmile 2
MEP Smile Centre
ILEA Learning Resources Branch
275 Kennington Lane
London
SE11 5QZ

Newman College
Genners Lane
Bartley Green
Birmingham
B32 3NT

NORICC
Northern Micromedia
Newcastle Polytechnic
Coach Lane Campus
Newcastle
NE7 7XA

RESOURCE
Exeter Road
off Coventry Grove
Wheatley
Doncaster
DN2 4TY

SMILE
Middle Row School
Kensall Row
London
W10 5DB

Anita Straker
Mundays
St Mary Bourne
nr Andover
Hants
SP11 6AY

Tecmedia Ltd
5 Granby Street
Loughborough
Leicestershire
LE11 3DU

Subject index

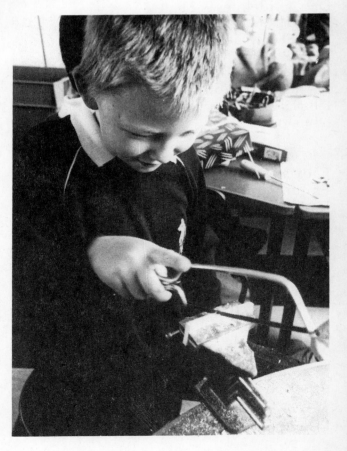

About the authors

After war service, **Geoffrey Matthews** taught in schools for 18 years before becoming the organiser of the first Nuffield Mathematics Teaching Project for five- to thirteen-year-olds. When the project ended, he was appointed as the first Professor of Mathematics Education in the country, occupying the Shell Chair at the Centre for Science Education, Chelsea College, London University. He was concerned with a number of other projects including EME (Early Mathematics Experience for three- to five-year-olds) which he co-directed with his wife Julia. He has written extensively on mathematics education and acted as presenter/adviser to a number of TV programmes. He is past president of the Mathematical Association and is now Emeritus Professor of London University.

Julia Matthews, the author of 'Structuring your programme', was headteacher of an Inner London infant/nursery school for many years. She co-directed a School Council Project on 'Early Mathematical Experiences' and at present has a research fellowship at the Froebel Educational Institute. In 1982 she obtained her doctorate with a study of the difficulties encountered by six- to seven-year-olds in written subtraction.

She believes firmly in the importance of laying good mathematical foundations and that this can be best achieved in a friendly atmosphere with the mathematics related to the children's other activities.

Julia Matthews is very experienced in all aspects of maths teaching.

172

Beryl Webber and **Jean Haigh** have written three chapters – 'Maths within the curriculum', 'Children as investigators' and 'Developing problem solving'.

Beryl Webber worked as an infant classroom teacher in Kent. During that time she became fascinated by the way young children learn mathematics. It was this interest which took her first to London University and then to Sussex to learn more about research methodology and children's learning to enable her to share her understanding with other teachers. By this time Beryl had become a member of the Kent Mathematics Advisory Team working on curriculum development projects and INSET. This work has now been extended to include initial teacher training at Christ Church College, Canterbury, where she is at present working as a lecturer/adviser.

Jean Haigh studied for her first degree in mathematics education at Portsmouth Polytechnic specialising in the middle years. She developed her interest through teaching mathematics for a short while in secondary schools and later in middle schools in Kent. She undertook further study at King's College, London, concentrating on why some children 'give up' immediately when faced with a difficulty in mathematics. She is now working as a teacher adviser in North-West Kent, involved in both mathematics in-service training and curriculum development.

Jean Haigh is a mathematics teacher adviser in North-West Kent.

Nicola Davies and **Vivienne Jahans** provide a refreshing approach in their chapter 'Presenting results'.

Nicola is a writer specialising in mathematics. She has run workshops and courses in primary cross-curricular maths.

Vivienne is deputy head of Cherry Garden Primary School, Bristol. She is active in many maths working groups, as well as being involved in writing material for her LEA.

Martin Blows has played a major role in the effective use of computers in the primary school.

Martin Blows helps you to use the calculator and computer effectively in the classroom in his chapter 'New technology'.

He is the headteacher at Race Leys Middle School, Bedworth, Warks, and a member of the Maths Association sub-committee looking at the integration of the calculator in the primary maths curriculum. He has run courses for teachers in both primary and secondary education on the use of the calculator, and played a major part in writing Warwickshire's *Primary Calculator Guide*. He is also involved with in-service work on the use of computers in primary education.

'Evaluating children's progress' was written by **Lesley Jones**. Lesley is a senior lecturer in primary education at Goldsmith's College, London University, where she is responsible for co-ordinating the BEd mathematics course. Before she moved to her present post she taught at both primary and secondary levels in Birmingham as well as doing some in-service work. She gained BPhil (Ed) and MEd degrees at Birmingham University, both of which are related to mathematics and mathematics teaching. She has written many articles for *Junior Education* and other publications. One of her main professional interests is in the area of girls and mathematics. She sees the development of language and discussion as an integral and vital part of primary mathematics.

Ruth Merttens, the author of 'Involving parents', is a senior lecturer in mathematics education at North London Polytechnic and is involved in both initial and in-service training of teachers. Previously she has taught across an age range from three to seventy and has written a series of activity books for parents and children, published by Octopus.

She is best known for her work running the IMPACT Project in which parents are involved in a structural way in their children's maths. IMPACT is currently running in three local education authorities – Barnet, Oxfordshire and Redbridge. It also incorporates a major research programme studying the effect of parental involvement on the children's mathematical development.

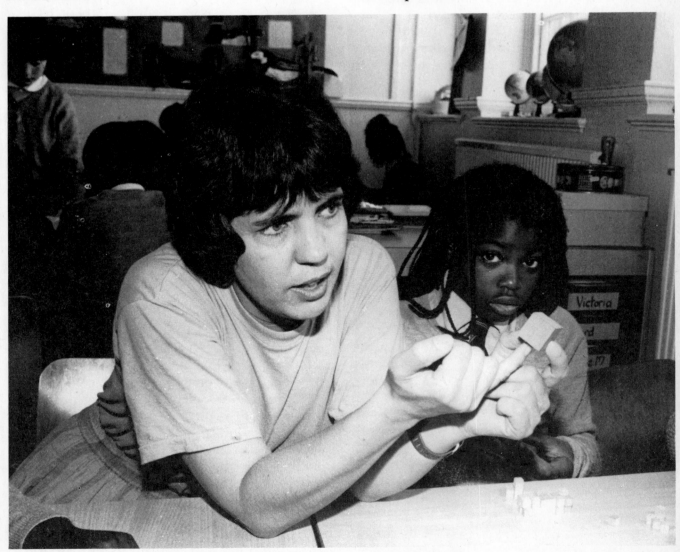

Lesley's main professional interest lies in the area of girls and mathematics.

Sally Dally, who wrote 'Catering for individual children', began teaching in 1970 and is now mathematics co-ordinator at Radford Semele CE Combined School, Leamington Spa, teaching eight- to twelve-year-olds. She worked in conjuction with the University of Warwick to produce the *Warwickshire Mathematics Project* in 1980 – a series of more than 100 worksheets plus teachers' handbook for the top 25 per cent of the ability range of 11 to 12-year-olds. Since 1981 she has taken part in much in-service work, lecturing and workshops on teaching the more able pupil.

Sally Dally has always played an active role in teaching the more able mathematics pupil.

Other Scholastic books

Bright Ideas titles

Previous titles in this series available are:

Bright Ideas Seasonal Activities
0 590 70831 7   £5.45

Bright Ideas Language Development
0 590 70834 1   £5.45

Bright Ideas Science
0 590 70833 3   £5.45

Bright Ideas Christmas Art and Craft
0 590 70832 5   £5.45

Bright Ideas Reading Activities
0 590 70535 0   £5.45

Bright Ideas Maths Activities
0 590 70534 2   £5.45

More Bright Ideas Christmas Art and Craft
0 590 70601 2   £5.45

Bright Ideas Classroom Management
0 590 70602 0   £5.45

Bright Ideas Games for PE
0 590 70690 X   £5.45

Bright Ideas Crafty Moneymakers
0 590 70689 6   £5.45

Bright Ideas Music
0 590 70700 0   £5.45

Bright Ideas Assemblies
0 590 70693 4   £5.45

Bright Ideas Writing
0 590 70701 9   £5.45

Bright Ideas Lifesavers
0 590 70694 2   £5.45

Bright Ideas Christmas Activities
0 590 70803 1   £5.45

Bright Ideas Spelling
0 590 70802 3   £5.45

Bright Ideas History
0 590 70804 X   £5.45

Teacher Handbooks titles

Titles in this series available are:

Teacher Handbooks Reading
0 590 70691 8   £7.95

Teacher Handbooks Language Resources
0 590 70692 6   £7.95

Teacher Handbooks Putting on a Performance
0 590 70801 5   £7.95

Write to Scholastic Publications Ltd, Westfield Road, Southam, Leamington Spa, Warwickshire CV33 0JH. Enclose your remittance. Make cheques payable to Scholastic Publications Ltd.